Light Up the Learning Brain *earns every star possible for this stellar contribution to the literature and conversation about raising, nurturing, and loving our youngsters.*

Pete Hall
Former School Principal & Author of *Always Strive to Be a Better You*

This book is an essential guide for educators to understand and apply brain-based methods in their classrooms. Seriously, Light Up the Learning Brain *should be in the hands of every educator.*

Byron McClure, D.Ed
Best-Selling Author of *Hacking Deficit Thinking*

Jessica Sinarski seamlessly translates complex brain theories into actionable insights for educators. The visuals, practicality, resources, and much more make this book remarkable!

Mathew Portell, M.Ed
Founder of the Trauma Informed Educators Network

Education CAN be magic and this book is an invaluable resource to help make the magic happen...a must-read for all educators!

Chele Gillon
District Lead Counselor

Light Up the Learning Brain *is a thoughtful, refreshing guide for new teachers and seasoned veterans alike.*

David Flink
Founder of Eye to Eye & Author of *Thinking Differently*

Light Up the Learning Brain *is a beacon of hope...I wholeheartedly endorse this book for its practicality, relevance, and the positive impact it can have on classrooms around the world.*

Whitney Jenkins
Elementary School Principal

Jessica has created an amazing foundation for educators to rethink behavior from carrots and sticks to brain-aligned teaching. This is a valuable addition to the library of every educator.

Joe Brummer
Author of *Building a Trauma-Informed Restorative School*

This book is going to improve the lives of so many teachers and students. It is a must for anyone and everyone who works with children.

Liliana Igmen
Assistant Principal & Special Education Coordinator

You will leave this book feeling validated, encouraged, and equipped to continue doing the beautiful work of educating the precious humans of the world.

Rachel Cullen, PhD
High School AP English Teacher

Jessica Sinarski has written a must read for educators and parents. It is user friendly, informative, and full of practical strategies.

Stephanie Josephson
Speech Language Therapist & Early Intervention Provider

This book is a game changer for teachers, counselors, principals, and parents.

Lori Downs
Student Assistance Coordinator

Sinarski's book is an emotional decision-making toolbox for all kids and their parents. Plain and simple, this book should be taught in schools.

Kate Evans
High School Language Arts Teacher

7 KEYS TO REDUCING DISRUPTIVE BEHAVIOR IN THE CLASSROOM

LIGHT UP
THE LEARNING
BRAIN

Duplication and Copyright

NATIONAL CENTER for
YOUTH ISSUES
P.O. Box 22185
Chattanooga, TN 37422-2185
423.899.5714 • 866.318.6294
fax: 423.899.4547 • www.ncyi.org

ISBN: 9781931636520
E-book ISBN: 9781931636537
Library of Congress Control Number: 2023922766
© 2023 National Center for Youth Issues, Chattanooga, TN
All rights reserved.
Written by: Jessica Sinarski
Published by National Center for Youth Issues
Printed in the U.S.A. • January 2024

This book is for the cycle breakers, the game changers, the courageous leaders and consensus builders, the worker bees, and the visionaries who know that education can be magic.

Let's go light up the learning brain!

CONTENTS

INTRODUCTION.. 9

The Problem

The Solution

How to Use this Book

PART ONE: IT'S A BRAIN THING!

CHAPTER ONE: UNDER CONSTRUCTION 16

Brains Are Built from the Bottom Up

What's Trust Got to Do with It?

The Upstairs Brain Across the Ages

Brains Are Diverse

Key Takeaways

Low-Stress Starting Point

CHAPTER TWO: THE BRAIN-BEHAVIOR CONNECTION

DEMYSTIFIED..31

Outside, Inside, and Between

The Mistrust Cycle

The Mistrusting Brain Goes to School

X-Ray Vision for the Downstairs Brain

Key Takeaways

Low-Stress Starting Point

CHAPTER THREE: FROM PROTECTION TO CONNECTION 45

Adverse Childhood Experiences (ACEs)
   and Trauma-Informed Practice

PCEs for Those ACEs: The Power
   of Positive Childhood Experiences

Post-Traumatic Wisdom

Hope for the Journey

Key Takeaways

Low-Stress Starting Point

PART TWO: KEYS TO UNLOCK STUDENT AND STAFF POTENTIAL

KEY ONE: BECOME A BRAIN BUILDER 61

Equip Your Staff
Empower Your Students
For the Adults at Home
The Building Blocks for Learning
Key Takeaways
Low-Stress Starting Point

KEY TWO: GET *ALL* THE SENSES INVOLVED 81

The Brain→Behavior→Senses Connection
We Have ~~Five~~ Eight Senses
Proprioception: The Secret System
    for Feeling Safe and in Control
The Senses and Self-Regulation
The Senses Go to School
Create a Sensory-Friendly School Setting
Trauma and the Senses
Key Takeaways
Low-Stress Starting Point

KEY THREE: PLAY AND BE PLAYFUL 101

Play, Connection, and Sensing Safety
Play for Social-Emotional Learning
Play to Learn Anything
Powerful Playful De-Escalation Strategies
Playful Tips and Scripts
Key Takeaways
Low-Stress Starting Point

KEY FOUR: BE CURIOUS 117

Get to Know Your Triggers
Glimmers and Anchors
Be Curious About Big Feelings
What Is the Need?
But What About Consequences?!
Bring Curiosity Home
Simple Scripts to Spark Curiosity
Key Takeaways
Low-Stress Starting Point

KEY FIVE: CREATE A CULTURE OF SAFETY 141

Felt Safety: The Brain Speaks Non-Verbal
Safety for Stressed Brains
Build Trust with Neurodivergent Students
Equity, Diversity, and a Culture of Belonging
Safety in Difficult Moments
Key Takeaways
Low-Stress Starting Point

KEY SIX: SHARE THE POWER... 159

Defiance, Disrespect, and the Downstairs Brain
Break Free from the Defense Brain Cycle
Cultivate Mutual Respect
Use and Coach Healthy Communication Strategies
Choose Support Over Control
Teach for True Learning
Key Takeaways
Low-Stress Starting Point

KEY SEVEN: LEAD WITH THE BRAIN IN MIND 177

Be a Brain-Building Leader
Be the Boss of Your Brain
See the Brain State Behind the Behavior
Lead with Compassion
Support Your Brain with Self-Compassion
Grief, Gratitude, and Grit
Key Takeaways
Low-Stress Starting Point

Conclusion.. 193
Glossary 194
Notes 200
About the Author 206
A Brief Look at Jessica's Sessions 207
About NCYI.. 208

Introduction

THE PROBLEM: BEHAVIORAL CHALLENGES GET IN THE WAY OF LEARNING

Educators, this book is for you. You got into this work to make the world a better place. Maybe it was the joy you felt when helping your brother learn to read, or the idea of shaping young minds. I have never met a teacher who said, "I really enjoy breaking up fights." I am guessing it's not your love of defiance that gets you out of bed in the morning, right?

A 2019 survey by the Education Advisory Board found an alarming increase in reported behavioral disruptions in early grades.[1] These tantrums, emotional outbursts, violent incidents, and episodes of defiance or shutdown impact the learning of all members of the classroom community. The pandemic's impact on the world of education has magnified these difficulties, making teaching even more demanding.

I have spent my career working with kids who have intense behavioral challenges. As a bright-eyed counselor in the South Bronx, I quickly realized I did *not* know what I needed to know to be effective in my job. So much hurt and hopelessness all around, and the great therapeutic skills I had learned in graduate school were not helping. As I work with educators across the country, I hear the same thing: we didn't learn what we needed to in school!

- What do I do when a kid tries to bite me?

- How do I teach algebra when a student suddenly runs out of my classroom?

- How do I create a culture of safety when stress levels are this high?

Questions like these set me on a path to learn *why* these behaviors are happening and what we can do about it. I found the answers in an unexpected place: brain science.

ALL BEHAVIOR COMES FROM THE BRAIN.

Now when I see extreme behaviors, I see a brain that is in survival mode. Unfortunately, when you are faced with behavior that comes from a brain working from that self-protective survival state, *your* brain and body naturally go there too. We end up in this pattern...

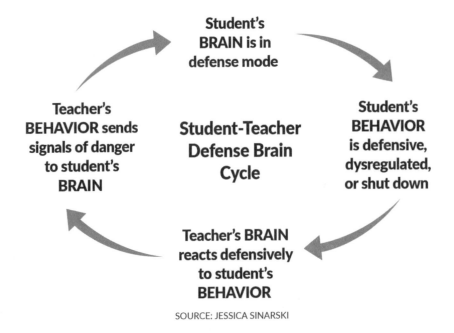

Student's BRAIN is in defense mode

Student's BEHAVIOR is defensive, dysregulated, or shut down

Teacher's BRAIN reacts defensively to student's BEHAVIOR

Teacher's BEHAVIOR sends signals of danger to student's BRAIN

Student-Teacher Defense Brain Cycle

SOURCE: JESSICA SINARSKI

When we are stuck in this cycle, there's not a lot of learning happening. And it's not because of bad kids and failing teachers. **It's a brain thing!**

It is easy to think of the brain as a lumpy pink blob. It is actually an intricate network of 70-100 billion neurons constantly sending and receiving signals through electrical and chemical messengers. You don't have to know all the details about this complex organ, but a little brain science can go a long way for educators.

THE SOLUTION: UNLOCK STUDENT (AND STAFF) POTENTIAL WITH SEVEN BRAIN-BASED KEYS

Many years ago, I was out to dinner with my husband and some work acquaintances. I don't recall how the topic came up, but I vividly remember the man to my right making some derogatory comments about the state of education in Brazil. "I don't know why teachers show up when the kids would rather be huffing gasoline than going to kindergarten."

My blood boiled. I had just begun working in a community much like the part of Brazil he was talking about, with families stuck in a cycle of poverty, systemic oppression, and marginalization. I snapped some sarcastic retort that I'm sure made no lasting impact on his worldview. What I knew then and still feel in every fiber of my being is this:

- No human comes into this world wanting to huff gasoline.
- No child, when feeling safe and loved, wants to be known as "the bad kid."
- No adolescent, when their needs are met in a culturally competent classroom, wants to pick fights and flunk out. There's stuff behind that. And while it is not your job as an

educator to solve all your students' problems, you *can* be a powerful part of the solution by working from a brain-based perspective.

Your school days don't have to be an endless cycle of frustration and dysregulation. Just as I knew those truths about students, I also know that no teacher wants to spend their day scolding, arguing, and kicking kids out of class. You want to help students *learn*!

One of the best parts of my work is seeing the anger, shame, and apathy lift as we put these brain-based keys in use—not by working *harder*, but by working *smarter*. Seeing the effectiveness of these strategies restores hope. You know that teacher spark? The joy of supporting a student well? The thrill of a two-grade-level leap in one year? That's the feeling you get when you light up the learning brain!

HOW TO USE THIS BOOK

> To embrace complexity within this book, you will find callouts like this with additional tips and strategies to support your well-being and address common barriers to implementation.

I am here to make your job easier, not with a whole new program, but with simple language and practical tools that support the great work you are already doing. Scripts, visuals, activities, and reflection exercises for both student and educator await you in the pages ahead.

Part One: It's a Brain Thing! Start here to get a concise and easy-to-use framework for understanding how brains develop and why that matters in our schools. This is critical both for increasing learning *and* reducing the behavior that so often gets in the way.

Part Two: Keys to Unlock Student and Staff Potential. In this section, each key builds on the last, providing a user-friendly guide to translate neuroscience into action steps. Make the most of the material with reflection opportunities and downloadable resources for immediate use.

At the end of each chapter, you will find **"Key Takeaways"** and a **"Low-Stress Starting Point"** suggestion. These are included to light up *your* learning brain and give you some quick "wins" as you begin to implement these brain-building strategies.

There is no one-size-fits-all solution in the world of education. Your personality, skills, culture, strengths, and experiences will impact how you apply the principles you learn in this book. You will also find adaptations for different learning styles and options for various ages. I encourage you to enjoy this book with colleagues—as a whole staff journey, in smaller personal learning communities, or just with your teacher bestie. Ready to light up the learning brain? Let's go!

I'm so glad we're in this together!
—Jessica

PART ONE 1

IT'S A BRAIN THING!

I N THE PAGES AHEAD, you will be introduced to phrases like The Mistrust Cycle, Downstairs Brain Protectors, and "having a Porcupine moment." While these might seem like odd words to find in a book for K-12 educators, I have seen the transformative power of this framework not only in school districts across the country, but in correctional facilities, addiction recovery, psychiatric hospitals, the foster and adoptive community, and beyond. In addition to helpful graphics and visuals, you will find real-life stories to bring the learning to life (note: all names and identifying information have been changed). Most of all, you will gain a user-friendly, trauma-sensitive, diversity-affirming understanding of the brain-behavior connection that I have seen literally change lives.

CHAPTER ONE

UNDER CONSTRUCTION

There is a simple way of understanding the brain that I hope makes into every classroom, home, workplace, government office, and beyond. The "house model of the brain" was first introduced in the book *The Whole-Brain Child*. According to authors Siegel and Bryson, the brain has two main operating systems, the Upstairs Brain and Downstairs Brain.[2] They also highlighted a part of the brain that is sometimes known as the "alarm system," "traffic director," "watchdog," or emotional center of the brain: the amygdala. Let's look at how these important parts of the brain develop and what that means for you in the classroom.

> *...the brain has two main operating systems, the Upstairs Brain and Downstairs Brain.*

BRAINS ARE BUILT FROM THE BOTTOM UP

Brain development is all about *connections*—inside and out. Billions of neurons, the brain cells responsible for sending and receiving messages, have to form connections for us to learn and grow.

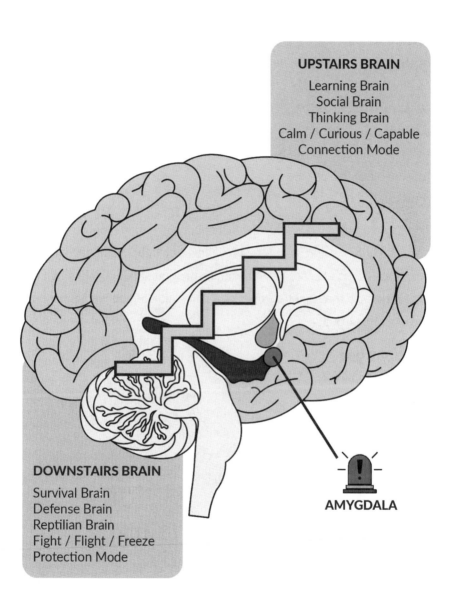

UPSTAIRS BRAIN

Learning Brain
Social Brain
Thinking Brain
Calm / Curious / Capable
Connection Mode

DOWNSTAIRS BRAIN

Survival Brain
Defense Brain
Reptilian Brain
Fight / Flight / Freeze
Protection Mode

AMYGDALA

Downstairs Brain: Protection Mode

The Downstairs Brain is the operating system online at birth. It works hard to keep us alive. It is responsible for basic functions like breathing and heartbeat. You may have heard it called "survival brain," "defense mode," or "the reptilian brain."

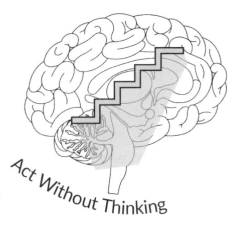

Act Without Thinking

The Downstairs Brain acts without thinking. It is the home of primal emotions and instincts as well as our fight-flight-freeze reactions. It also favors power and control over cooperation, a characteristic that will be important to remember as we move through this book.

Upstairs Brain: Connection Mode

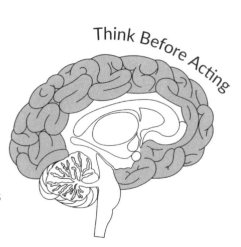

Think Before Acting

The Upstairs Brain is made up of the full outer portion of the brain called the cerebral cortex. Unlike its quick-responding counterpart, this advanced network of neurons develops slowly, not reaching full maturity (i.e. optimal connection) until the mid-twenties. It includes the most advanced portion of the brain, the prefrontal cortex, which helps us manage the planning, problem-solving, and perseverance required in adulthood. The Upstairs Brain is also where our "social-approach/

engagement" system lives.[3] It lets us play, enjoy the company of others, share, create healthy community, and care for others.

The Upstairs Brain thinks before acting. It is the home of our calm, curious, collaborative choices. When the Upstairs Brain is in charge, we can make thoughtful decisions, regulate our big feelings, wrestle with complexity, develop insight, control impulses, and change habits. Teaching, parenting, and "adulting" in general requires a tremendous amount of Upstairs Brain power.

Amygdala: The Alarm System & Gatekeeper

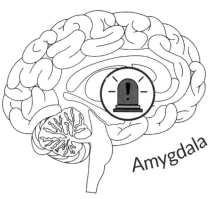

Millions of tiny bits of information hit the brain every second, and the amygdala has to make a lightning-fast decision about each data point. Its essential question is always *Am I safe? -OR- Am I in danger (physically, emotionally, or relationally)?* The amygdala's answer to that question, in milliseconds, determines whether the Upstairs Brain can run the show or if that Downstairs Brain survival mode needs to be in control.

Genes provide the basic blueprint for brain development, but prenatal and early life experiences have a profound impact on what part of the "house" gets more attention.[4] For the amygdala to give the Upstairs Brain the "all-clear" signal it needs to grow and develop, we need to know that our cries and smiles matter.

Why talk about infant brain development in a book for educators? There are oh-so-many reasons, but the top three are: (1) Behavior you see in the classroom may be related to much earlier experiences in a child's life. To keep your Upstairs Brain engaged, it helps to know that. This book will also equip you with what to do with that knowledge. (2) You were an infant once too. We cannot change the past, but I have found that understanding why we do what we do often helps us find our way forward. (3) While infancy is the most prolific time of brain development, childhood and adolescence are significant brain-building times as well. Understanding how brains grow and mature will help you help your students...and make your job easier along the way.

WHAT'S TRUST GOT TO DO WITH IT?

The Downstairs Brain is fully furnished at birth, ready to kick into action with cries of distress at every little need. Hungry? The newborn baby will cry until fed. Tired? Fuss until asleep. Gas bubble in the tummy? Speaking from experience, expect hours of wailing until that little toot brings relief. The Upstairs Brain, on the other hand, is still very much under construction, littered with tools and gaping holes in the structure that will take another 25+ years to complete. So how does that brain house get built? It's all about relationship!

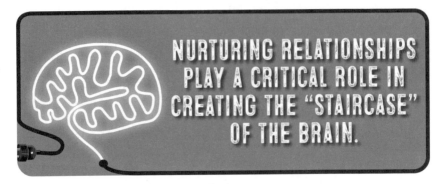

NURTURING RELATIONSHIPS PLAY A CRITICAL ROLE IN CREATING THE "STAIRCASE" OF THE BRAIN.

The Harvard Center for the Developing Child highlights responsive caregiving as a vital element in making connections in the developing brain.[5] In other words, nurturing relationships play a critical role in creating the "staircase" of the brain. This is part

The Downstairs Brain is fully furnished at birth.

of The Trust-Building Cycle that begins in infancy, where a baby moves between distress and relief, from dysregulation to relaxation thanks to the attentive care of a parent or caregiver.

The Trust-Building Cycle

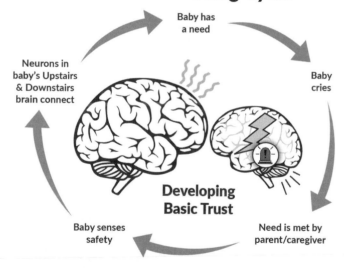

SOURCE: JESSICA SINARSKI AND DR. JONATHAN BAYLIN

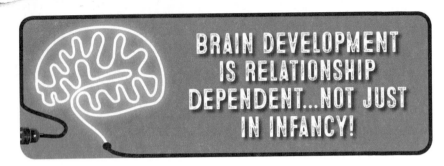

BRAIN DEVELOPMENT IS RELATIONSHIP DEPENDENT...NOT JUST IN INFANCY!

An attentive caregiver takes cues from the infant about what is needed in the moment. And what is the main cue? Cries! Adults' responses to an infant's distress play a critical role in whether that little brain has the safety and energy it needs to work on Upstairs Brain construction.

Responsive caregiving also involves lots of "serve-and-return" interactions, those back-and-forth volleys about everyday life that show that you are interested in the child's world. Seven-year-old Molly Wright provides some great insight on this in her TED Talk "How every child can thrive by five."[6] She begins with the question: "What if I was to tell you that a game of peek-a-boo could change the world?" Playful, caring attention from a parent or caregiver in the earliest years of life has a lasting impact on the developing brain. Play continues to be a power tool for building Upstairs Brain capacity. More on that in Part Two!

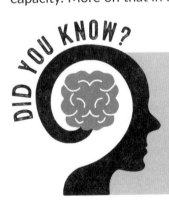

DID YOU KNOW?

When talking with someone, nonverbal cues like facial expression, tone of voice, and body posture are processed by the brain much more quickly than the words themselves.

Remember this viral video? Beyond melting our hearts, comedian DJ Pryor and his son Kingston were demonstrating the trust-building power of serve-and-return communication.[7] The words mean nothing, but that little boy's brain is "hearing" from his dad's tone of voice, attention, and warm gaze that he, Kingston, matters! I can

SOURCE: HTTPS://YOUTU.BE/AY35EXTKVLY

just see the neurons connecting in his brain, the staircase getting stronger, the tools in action in that rudimentary Upstairs Brain.

THE UPSTAIRS BRAIN ACROSS THE AGES

I was learning this science right as I became a mom. It has been fascinating to watch my children's development through a brain-based lens. Sometimes I feel like I can *see* their brains growing. While I still have all the normal frustrations of parenting, I also have a lot of compassion for what they can and cannot do (yet!), as well as what they need from me and other safe adults in their lives. I'm hoping this table will give you a better picture of what the Upstairs Brain under construction looks like. I have incorporated some of Erik Erikson's theory of psychosocial development into this as well to help bring each developmental stage to life.[8]

As you look over these ages and stages, it is important to keep in mind that many factors impact when particular skills develop. Every brain has different strengths and areas of needed support. In other words, brains are diverse.

APPROXIMATE AGE	DEVELOPMENTAL STAGE	UPSTAIRS BRAIN DEVELOPMENT	WHAT IT MIGHT LOOK LIKE
0-18 months	Trust vs. Mistrust	• Learning that my smiles and cries matter • Finding ways to get my needs met with my safe adults	• Laughing and babbling • Beginning to ask for things with gestures and sounds • Crying during transitions • Coming back to calm after getting upset
Toddler	Autonomy vs. Shame & Doubt	• Exploding curiosity • Language acquisition • Increasing body awareness	• Exploring my world with all my senses • Testing limits • Asking questions • Repeating words and phrases • Potty training • Curiosity about body parts
Preschool	Initiative vs. Guilt	• Curiosity and courage to try new things • Increasing understanding of structure, roles, and rules • Growing creativity • Sequencing and beginning to understand cause and effect • Beginning to identify basic emotions	• "I can do it!" attitude • Mimicking what I see • Imaginative play • Playing to make sense of my environment and experiences • Skill building with support through frustrating attempts • More goal-directed actions like arts & crafts, learning letters and numbers, etc.

Elementary	Industry (sense of competence) vs. Inferiority	• Building on foundational skills • Comparing myself with peers • Increasing self-control • More complex thinking • Understanding the feelings of others	• Learning to read and write • Exploring hobbies and interests • Questioning differences and similarities • Learning to be a team player • Taking responsibility for more classroom or household chores • Caring about others
Adolescent*	Identity vs. Confusion	• Learning I am my own person with different problems and successes than the adults in my life • Gaining skills for adult roles • Increasing capacity for complex thought and reasoning	• Connecting with available supports, like peers and trusted adults for guidance • Managing more responsibilities • Taking on leadership roles or employment opportunities • Finding my own style, interests, priorities, and passions • Exploring personal values that differ from my family of origin
Young Adult*	Intimacy vs. Isolation	• Becoming my own person • Deepening relationships and connections with myself and others	• Navigating life with others (roommates, colleagues, etc.) • Enjoying the reciprocal nature of healthy relationships • Dealing with the emotional ups and downs of adult life • Making big decisions about my future

*The adolescent and young adult stages overlap. Both identity formation and the development of close personal relationships are critical during these transitional years.

BRAINS ARE DIVERSE

Your differences are your strengths, and society needs everything that makes you you.

– Mickey Rowe, An Autistic Broadway Actor's Transformational Insights

THERE IS NO ONE "RIGHT" WAY OF THINKING, LEARNING, COMMUNICATING, AND BEHAVING.

The term "neurodiversity" was coined by Australian sociologist Judy Singer to promote equality and inclusion of those in the autistic community and others with neurological differences. Since the brain controls behavior, and as many as one in five people in the U.S. are neurodivergent, this is a critically important topic for educators.[9] According to Dr. Nicole Baumer, a neurodevelopmental disabilities specialist and neurology instructor at Harvard Medical School, neurodiversity helps us understand that:

1. People experience and interact with the world in different ways,

2. There is no "right" way of thinking, learning, communicating, and behaving,

3. Differences are not deficits.[10]

Learning style, communication, processing, and the way people are misunderstood or misjudged by others are all impacted by neurodivergent identities like dyslexia, dyspraxia, fetal alcohol spectrum disorders (FASD), and autism.[11] While you have likely heard these words in terms of diagnoses, it is important to note that diagnoses, particularly in the mental health field, are merely clusters of symptoms. Additionally, Western medicine tends to have a deficit model, focusing on what is *wrong* with you by labeling diseases or disorders. I'm not saying diagnoses or labels are inherently bad. Sometimes a diagnosis is validating: "Oh! That's why X thing is so hard for me." But as with all complicated human things, how it is done matters. The tools in this book will help you bring a compassionate, brain-based lens to your work with neurodiverse students (and staff).

I live in a home of neurodivergence, both in my kids and my partner. Honestly, it is easy for my Downstairs Brain to kick in and notice the negative; the tasks that didn't get done or the impulsivity that lands us in the emergency room. But that's not the whole story! I was listening to a podcast a few years ago about Attention-Deficit Hyperactivity Disorder (ADHD), which the guest described as having an "explorer brain." What a refreshing perspective! It was the reminder I needed to notice the strengths in my differently-wired family, the fun and spontaneity that my rule-averse husband brings, the joy of dancing in the kitchen even though there are chores to be done, and the unique perspective that my son's dyslexia brings to our dinnertime conversations.

In their book *Hacking Deficit Thinking*, school psychologists McClure and Reed encourage readers to "cultivate communities of admiration and collaboration where we don't just 'accept' and 'include' people *despite* their differences, but rather admire them *because* of their differences."[12] Community-building, admiration, collaboration, perspective-taking—these are all only possible if we engage our own Upstairs Brains so that we can light up all the diverse styles of learning brains in our students.

DID YOU KNOW?

Fetal Alcohol Spectrum Disorders (FASD) impact 2-5% of the U.S. population.[13] With compassion for mamas who were fed the lie that a little bit won't hurt or who were drinking to cope with their own trauma, this statistic means that as many as 1 in 20 students in our schools will struggle with self-regulation, executive function, mental health challenges, and learning differences due to FASD. Because of the stigma involved and lack of research and funding, proper diagnosis and treatment are rare. Thankfully, the same trust-building strategies that help other neurodivergent students and all the brain-building tools in this book are helpful for kids impacted by fetal alcohol and drug exposure as well. To learn more, visit www.apa.org/monitor/2022/07/news-fetal-alcohol-syndrome.

KEY TAKEAWAYS

- The brain has two main operating systems:
  - The Downstairs Brain is in charge of basic functions like breathing and heartbeat. It also is the home of primal emotions, quick reactions, survival responses, and the need for power and control.
  - The Upstairs Brain lets us think before we act. In addition to helping regulate the big feelings coming from the Downstairs Brain, this more advanced portion of the brain lets us play,

connect with others, wrestle with complexity, and navigate life as an adult.

- Our brains are designed to act before thinking, especially in the early years of child development.

- Nurturing, responsive relationships in the early years help clear the path for more Upstairs Brain development.

- No two brains are identical. Better understanding the neurodivergent community's ways of thinking, learning, communicating, and behaving honors the much-needed variety of any healthy society.

LOW-STRESS STARTING POINT

Let's reflect...

Curiosity comes from the Upstairs Brain, so this first low-stress starting point is a short reflection exercise. Think of a recent interaction that left you feeling a strong emotion. Now bring some curiosity to the behavior of everyone involved.

- What parts of the brain do you think were active?

- Do you have a guess about why?

- How does that impact your view of the incident and/or what you might do next time?

CHAPTER TWO

THE BRAIN-BEHAVIOR CONNECTION DEMYSTIFIED

All behavior comes from the brain.

Let me say that again: All behavior comes from the brain.

What does that mean for you and me? If we are trying to prevent or mitigate challenging *behavior*, it will help if we understand more about the brain!

OUTSIDE, INSIDE, AND BETWEEN

Let's start by looking at where the brain gets its information: outside, inside, and between.

OUTSIDE: The Five Senses

What am I experiencing from my sense of touch, smell, taste, hearing, and sight?

INSIDE: The Three Hidden Senses

What is my vestibular system detecting about balance and movement?

What proprioceptive input is coming from my muscles and joints?

What body clues is my interoception detecting from my gut and other organs?

BETWEEN: Interpersonal Cues

What am I picking up from your eyes, tone of voice, and body language?

WE NEED EACH OTHER. DESPERATELY.

We will spend a whole chapter on our *eight* senses that transmit information from OUTSIDE and INSIDE. For now, it is important to pay attention to the word BETWEEN. Western culture often values the individualist, "lone ranger," I'll-do-it-on-my-own mentality. I get it! I am an entrepreneur and go-getter, but the reality remains: we need each other. Desperately. One thing I have learned from twenty years as a trauma therapist is that the kids who need us most usually tell us in confusing, even hurtful ways. This is true with adults too! When we look with a brain-based lens, though, even the wackiest, most extreme behaviors start to make sense. Did this person feel lots of relief and relaxation in the early years from thousands of trips through The Trust-Building Cycle? Or has the protection of mistrust, for whatever reason, been more adaptive?

> *...the kids who need us most usually tell us in confusing, even hurtful ways.*

If you are thinking, "Wait, this is sounding a little too 'therapy-ish' to me," don't worry! See, if my therapist hat was on, I would never tell you how to feel.

You do not have to be your students' therapist, parent, or best friend. You do not have to create intense personal relationships with all 200 11th graders in your English lit classes to be successful as a teacher. You do have to bring your Upstairs Brain into your work if you want to help your students succeed. Fortunately, there are lots of non-"therapy-ish" ways to do that!

THE MISTRUST CYCLE

What does "mistrust" have to do with your work as an educator? To understand this next part, I'm going to share the stories of Josie and Kyle. Both came to see me with similar symptoms: angry outbursts, disrupted relationships, low frustration tolerance, quick to shut down, struggles with the activities of daily life, anxiety, and depressed mood. If we could use some x-ray vision, I imagine their brains looked a lot like this:

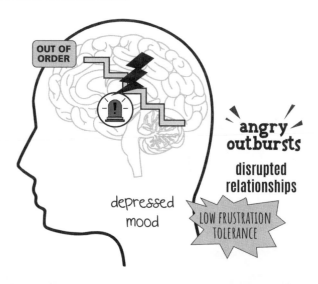

OUT OF ORDER

angry outbursts

disrupted relationships

depressed mood

LOW FRUSTRATION TOLERANCE

Josie was born into a family that had the deck stacked against them: a parent dealing with undiagnosed mental illness, several children, and not a lot of supports. As the youngest, Josie didn't get a lot of attention. Food was scarce. Affection was infrequent. This was a kiddo who learned very quickly that her cries and smiles didn't matter. Josie bounced around homes, living with friends or neighbors as her parents tried to make ends meet. These experiences further reinforced that she was not safe, not important, and the only way to get her needs met was to stay vigilant, working hard to please those around her. As she approached adulthood, she ended up in an abusive relationship, deepening the lesson that people can't be trusted to care for her. She experienced this cycle repeatedly, both as a baby, and throughout her formative years:

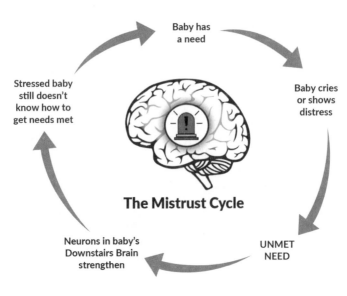

SOURCE: JESSICA SINARSKI

No wonder Josie was struggling! But Kyle's story is quite different. He was born into a family that was excited for his arrival and ready to pour out love and affection on him. Yet something seemed off. Kyle was fussy all the time. Mom tried everything, but the screaming continued. Over the next few years, several food allergies were discovered that had been causing tremendous discomfort, but baby Kyle didn't have a way to tell his parents.

When I started working with Kyle at age six, it also became clear that he had sensory processing difficulties that were creating even more distress and dysregulation. His parents were doing everything they knew to do, but his body and brain were still screaming out with unmet needs. This translated to not getting work done in class, having a short fuse with siblings and peers, and even screaming "I hate you" at his parents (and then melting in shame afterward). Not because he was a troublemaker. Not because his parents were bad. It's a brain thing!

His parents were doing everything they knew to do, but his body and brain were still screaming out with unmet needs.

When the amygdala keeps getting alarm signals, and crying or smiling hasn't relieved the stress, the Downstairs Brain will find another way. There is no time or energy to work on Upstairs Brain skill-building. This is a brain in survival mode, but without the most critical means of survival: connection.

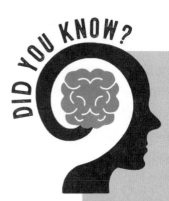

Loneliness and isolation are a major public health concern leading to an increased risk of premature death comparable to smoking.[14] According to the U.S. Surgeon General's 2023 report, research indicates all kinds of negative physical, emotional, and even educational outcomes from the growing levels of social isolation in our society. What is the cure? Social connection.[15]

THE MISTRUSTING BRAIN GOES TO SCHOOL

As you may have noticed from Josie and Kyle's stories, there are many reasons a baby might experience unmet needs leading to The Mistrust Cycle early in life (and negative consequences down the road). Here are just a few of the myriad things that can set a brain up to prioritize Downstairs Brain development:

- Parent is battling addiction or mental health issues and doesn't meet the need
- Baby's sensory system can't feel the soothing
- Medical issues prevent meeting the need (life-saving procedures are often quite traumatizing)
- Need is met inconsistently or with anger from a stressed parent
- Parent has experienced trauma and marginalization leading to their own unhealed time in The Mistrust Cycle
- Neurodivergence impacts baby's ability to feel "typical" relief

- Parent is distracted by devices and not attentive to the need
- Baby is separated from birth family
- Parent or caregiver doesn't know how to meet the need

Without care and support, a child stuck in The Mistrust Cycle will struggle with Upstairs Brain development. All their resources become devoted to their more primitive survival systems. That growing brain has learned that it cannot trust a safe grown-up to help, and whether or not this is true, every neuron is firing as if it were! In the classroom, it can be hard to see Downstairs Brain behavior as the survival mode that it is. This will become much clearer as you continue through this book. For now, here are a few common examples:

Examples of Downstairs Brain Behavior in the Classroom

ACTIVE DEFENSE (Fight or Flight)	IMMOBILE DEFENSE (Freeze or Shut Down/ Collapse)
Arguing or yelling	Ignoring requests
Constantly in motion	Daydreaming
Running from the room	Head down on desk
Picking fights	Refusing to answer

Remember, our brains are either in connection mode, with the Upstairs Brain calling the shots, or in protection mode, with the amygdala shouting, "DANGER! DANGER!" That's when the "Act Without Thinking" team from the Downstairs Brain runs the show.

"Why did you leave off the term 'Fawn?'" While it is important to understand that perfectionism and people-pleasing can be a survival response just as much as fighting or shutting down, the term "fawn" has a subservient connotation that many trauma survivors find off-putting. Check out "Chameleon moments" in the next section for another take on this important concept.

X-RAY VISION FOR THE DOWNSTAIRS BRAIN

The use of animal metaphors for thinking about the Downstairs Brain has been tremendously helpful, not just to young children, but even to teens and adults. Recently, after sharing this framework with a group of educators in Georgia, a high school teacher came up to me and said, "This gives me a lot to process. I think I have had whole Downstairs Brain days. And weeks and months." This played out in negative interactions with his high school students, and he was realizing it didn't have to be that way!

There are four Downstairs Brain Protectors that live in each of us and getting to know your *own* "Act Without Thinking" team is an essential step on the journey to become the boss of your brain and empower others to do the same. This excerpt from *Your Amazing Brain* offers a little peek inside.

The brain pays a lot of attention to one big question: Am I safe? At the slightest hint of danger, feeling left out, or even just something you don't like, your amygdala is ready to send in your Downstairs Brain Protectors. INTRODUCING...

If you find yourself thinking, "*This is the worst,*" "*I don't need you,*" "*I don't waaaaant to,*" or just generally complaining about everything, you might be having a Porcupine moment.

If you find yourself yelling, threatening, internally raging, or thinking, "*That kid is the worst,*" you might be having a Tiger moment.

Are you trying to please others or be just like them? If you find yourself thinking, *"I can't do anything right"* or *"I'm the worst,"* you might be having a Chameleon moment.

If you find your thoughts and emotions shutting down or feel like you are in a fog and can't ask for help, you might be having a Turtle moment.

COMMON DOWNSTAIRS BRAIN "PROTECTION MODE" EXAMPLES ACROSS AGES

	PRESCHOOL	K-5TH	6TH-12TH	TEACHER AND ADMIN
Porcupine Moment	• Whining • "No!" • Excluding others	• Snapping at others • Teasing • "I don't want to" • Keeping others away • Gossiping or other clique-y behavior	• Arms crossed • Grumpy shrug • Talking back • Avoiding social events • "Whatever" • "This is stupid"	• Guarded posture • Avoiding eye contact • Furrowed brow • Complain and blame • Taking behavior personally • Getting sucked into a negative group mindset
Tiger Moment	• Biting • Spitting • Hitting • Tantrums • Kicking • Screaming	• Arguing • Yelling • Quick temper • Running out of the classroom (often turns into a Turtle moment) • Rough with others • Talking meanly about others • Name calling	• Fighting • Cyberbullying • Slamming doors • Posturing or pacing • Purposely bumping others in the hallway • "I hate this" • Swearing at others • Extreme violent talk	• Getting in someone's face • Threatening • Yelling • Intimidating posture • Command and demand mode • Holds power over staff/students • Demeaning/labeling students or staff • Attacking others online
Chameleon Moment	• Hiding behind a parent • Hesitant to join in play	• Embarrassed by attention • "I can't do anything right" • Freezing when asked a question	• Following peer pressure • Driven by social media • Difficulty hearing positives • Perfectionism • "I suck at everything"	• Afraid to show "the real me" • Nervous to speak up • Needing to be liked by everyone • Looking for acceptance on social media
Turtle Moment	• Hiding when in trouble • Withdrawing from the group • Blank stare	• Not wanting to go to school • Avoiding homework • Going on YouTube a lot	• Cutting class • Head down on desk • Hiding in hoodie • Daydreaming • Checked out • Phone scrolling • Missing assignments • Stuck and seems to refuse solutions	• "Why should I even try?" • Numb • Detached • No pleasure in teaching • Zoning out • Mindless scrolling

*As with all these Downstairs Brain moments, sometimes this is a needed form of protection. This is especially true for marginalized populations who have had to mask their neurodivergent preferences, hide their gender identity, or use other protective Chameleon survival strategies for navigating unfair power dynamics.

Behaviors coming from these protective parts of our nervous system, AKA "Downstairs Brain moments," are incredibly common. We all have them. Every day. Our Tiger and Turtle Protectors have the best of intentions, but without some Upstairs Brain support they end up instigating hurt, miscommunication, burnout, and despair. In fact, one of the main jobs of the Upstairs Brain is regulating the big feelings and primal instincts coming from the Downstairs Brain. This is a skill that grows over time with lots of support from someone else's Upstairs Brain!

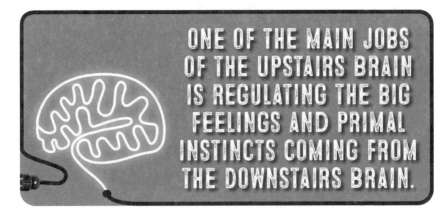

ONE OF THE MAIN JOBS OF THE UPSTAIRS BRAIN IS REGULATING THE BIG FEELINGS AND PRIMAL INSTINCTS COMING FROM THE DOWNSTAIRS BRAIN.

Brains in protection mode have a way of setting each other off. It takes a lot of Upstairs Brain power to not respond to a student's "Porcupine moment" with a Tiger or Turtle moment of your own! This is why it is so important for us to get to know the *whole* brain, including the "Act Without Thinking" team that can get extra protective. As Dr. Dan Siegel writes in *Pocket Guide to Interpersonal Neurobiology*, "By envisioning the brain, people become empowered to make changes in their lives with more efficacy and self-compassion."[16] We'll talk more about self-compassion later, but I *know* you wouldn't be reading this book if you didn't want to be more effective at your job. Keeping the brain in mind is an important part of breaking free from the Student-Teacher Defense Brain Cycle, empowering us to move from protection mode to connection mode.

KEY TAKEAWAYS

- The brain "decides" what to do based on information from three places.
  - OUTSIDE – the five senses (touch, smell, taste, hearing, and sight)
  - INSIDE – three hidden senses (vestibular, proprioception, and interoception)
  - BETWEEN – interpersonal cues (especially eyes, tone of voice, and body language)
- The Mistrust Cycle can lead to classroom behaviors like yelling, running away, ignoring requests, and picking fights.
- There are lots of reasons someone may have spent time in The Mistrust Cycle. Piling on shame and blame won't help break the cycle.

- The brain's tendency to default to "protection mode" can be better understood through the lens of Porcupine, Tiger, Chameleon, and Turtle moments, which are common at all ages of development, including adulthood.

LOW-STRESS STARTING POINT

Let's reflect...

Think about your day or week. Can you identify a time you had one of these "Downstairs Brain moments?"

What helped you get your Upstairs Brain back in charge?

What insights does that give you, perhaps to make a small change or try a different way to handle a similar situation in the future?

FROM PROTECTION TO CONNECTION

By now, you may be appreciating the enormity of what can send our brains into protection mode. The good news is, brains can change! Even if the survival-mode team has gotten strong, connection mode is in there. Underneath those Porcupine spikes and stealthy Chameleon skills is a desire to be safe, seen, and valued. The cries might sound a lot more like Tiger rage, and the smiles may be hidden deep inside a Turtle shell, but I promise you this: every student and staff member and parent in your school community longs to know that their smiles and cries matter.

> If you're not sure that your cries and smiles mattered when you were little, it may be difficult to imagine providing that kind of care and attention to others under the fluorescent lights of your school building. I am hoping this book will make it a lot easier! I also encourage you to talk it out with someone you trust, such as a supportive colleague, mentor, therapist, or wise friend. We adults need each other too! It's a brain thing.

ADVERSE CHILDHOOD EXPERIENCES (ACES) AND TRAUMA-INFORMED PRACTICE

One of the biggest myths we need to bust is that if you have experienced childhood adversity there's nothing we can do about it.

– Nadine Burke Harris, M.D.

"Why 'trauma-informed?' I heard we should be trauma-sensitive or trauma-responsive." As long as you are not trauma-ignorant or trauma-inducing, it doesn't matter which words we use here. Let's just keep doing the work!

Trauma has become a prominent part of the conversation in education, as well it should. Unfortunately, that can also lead to so much discussion that it begins to feel like no more than the latest buzzword or topic *du jour* that will soon be forgotten. I have spent the last 20 years supporting kids and adults who survived significant abuse and neglect. I am not in agreement with calling everything "trauma" or with the ways that neuroscience has been misused and confused in the world of education. Instead, I am here to share a trauma-sensitive understanding of the brain-body connection that has completely changed my life: personally, professionally, and for the kids, parents, and professionals I have the honor of coming alongside.

The study of early life trauma and the impact on brain and body is still quite new as a scientific field. As such, there are dozens of versions of what being "trauma-informed" means. In their book,

What Happened to You?: Conversations on Trauma, Resilience, and Healing, authors Bruce Perry and Oprah Winfrey state that trauma-informed practice is **"approaching people with the awareness that 'what happened to you' is important, that it influences your behavior and your health. And then using that awareness to act accordingly and respond appropriately."**[17]

Any discussion of trauma-informed education usually involves a quick recap of the original Adverse Childhood Experiences (ACEs) study first published in the American Journal of Preventive Medicine in 1998. The Centers for Disease Control and Prevention (CDC) partnered with Kaiser Permanente in southern California to have adults take a 10-question survey about potentially stressful or traumatic events in their childhood and compare the results with their individual health data. The number of "yes" answers to those 10 questions became known as the participant's "ACE score."

The Types of ACEs

ABUSE	NEGLECT	HOUSEHOLD DYSFUNCTION	
PHYSICAL	PHYSICAL	MENTAL ILLNESS	INCARCERATED PARENT
EMOTIONAL	EMOTIONAL	MOTHER TREATED VIOLENTLY	SUBSTANCE ABUSE
SEXUAL		DIVORCE	

There were a few staggering findings:

1. ACEs are incredibly common, even among the privileged group in the original study. The 17,337 participants were predominantly White (74.8%) and well-educated, with 75.2% reporting at least some college education. This study has been replicated and built upon over the years since, with more marginalized populations having even higher rates of adversity.

2. The higher the ACE score, the higher the risk for a whole host of poor physical and mental health outcomes, including depression, autoimmune disorders, heart disease, and diabetes.

3. An ACE score of 4 or more was correlated with a 20-year difference in life expectancy compared to those with an ACE score of 0. The CDC offers this pyramid model for understanding the path of trauma's impact on health and well-being.[18]

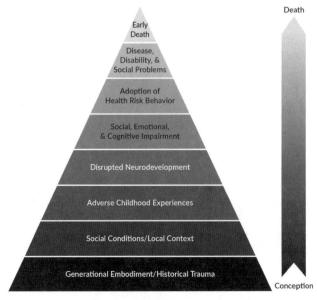

Mechanisim by which Adverse Childhood Experiences Influence Health and Well-being throughout the Lifespan

SOURCE: HTTPS://WWW.CDC.GOV/VIOLENCEPREVENTION/ACES/ABOUT.HTML

Dr. Nadine Burke Harris, author of the groundbreaking book *The Deepest Well*, has been a leader in putting the ACE's science into practice in the world of pediatric medicine. Through scientific rigor and compassionate writing, she helped bring to light how the body's survival response is both adaptive and damaging. Understanding this "both-and" reality has been powerful and freeing for many trauma survivors I have worked with over the years. Dr. Burke Harris also explained how patterns of behavior are tied to underlying biological mechanisms that were impacted by toxic levels of stress.[19] In other words, the protective brain-body response to trauma is in service of survival.

Therefore, viewed through the lens of trauma-informed practice, the CDC's pyramid looks more like this.

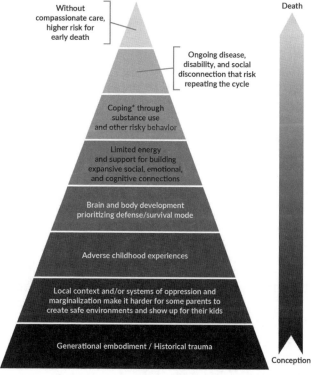

A Trauma-Informed Perspective on ACEs Imapct and Well-Being

SOURCE: CENTERS FOR DISEASE CONTROL AND PREVENTION
ACE PYRAMID UPDATED AND MODIFIED BY JESSICA SINARSKI

*Thanks to the RYSE Center for naming this reframe of "coping" and continuing the exploration of deeper meanings that can be found in data.

This is the point in most workshops with educators where I remind the group that ACEs are *fact not fate*.

I have an ACE score of 7, a fact that played a significant role in why I am so passionate about helping people understand trauma, the brain, and the path to healing. It's also where I bring up Positive Childhood Experiences (PCEs) and remind participants that, yes, early experiences impact brain development, but that is not the end of the story.

PCES FOR THOSE ACES: THE POWER OF POSITIVE CHILDHOOD EXPERIENCES

While there has been an understandable push for educators to be trained on the impact of ACEs, an often overlooked complementary field of study is Positive Childhood Experiences, or PCEs. In 2019, a team of researchers examined the impact of these seven PCEs on those impacted by adversity:[20]

- Felt able to talk to their family about feelings
- Felt their family stood by them during difficult times
- Enjoyed participating in community traditions
- Felt a sense of belonging in high school
- Felt supported by friends

- Had at least two non-parent adults who took genuine interest in them

- Felt safe and protected by an adult in their home

The results, published in the *Journal of the American Medical Association*, seem especially encouraging for teachers, counselors, and administrators. While you have very little impact on what goes on inside a child's home, you *can* be sure that all students' cultures are represented and celebrated so that kids can enjoy participating in community traditions. You can be one of at least two non-parent adults who take a genuine interest in a student. Secondary educators, you can help nurture a sense of belonging in high school. These are protective factors, even for kids experiencing adversity at home. And the buffering effects of these positive experiences are similarly powerful and cumulative. One 2019 study found that when ACE scores were moderate, PCEs largely neutralized the negative effects of ACEs on adult health.[21] Similarly, a 2021 article for the Academy of Criminal Justice Sciences found that high PCE scores were associated with decreased recidivism even in the face of high ACE scores.[22]

Additional PCE studies are confirming what we learned through the ACEs research: **Relationships matter.** I'm guessing this isn't the first time in your work as an educator that you have heard that relationships matter. Unfortunately, the Downstairs Brain can get in the way! When a staff member comes at you with their Tiger claws out or a student is in Turtle mode and seems beyond reach, it's only natural that your protection mode begins to kick in, making relationship-building that much more difficult. There are countless strategies ahead in this book to tend to *your* mind and heart so that you can build the relationships that will bring out the best in your students and staff.

POST-TRAUMATIC WISDOM

If you have been through a lot, please know that you are not alone. As I mentioned, Western medicine tends to focus on what's *wrong* with you instead of what is healthy and brilliant and strong. So, you have probably heard a lot more about Post-Traumatic Stress Disorder (PTSD) than you have about post-traumatic growth or wisdom. While the concept has existed long before this term was coined by researchers Tedeschi and Calhoun in 1996, "post-traumatic growth" refers to the personal strength, closer relationships, and other areas of development that someone might experience following a crisis or traumatic event.[23] "When you've lived through adversity, you can come to a point in your life where you can look back, reflect, learn, and grow from the experience," explains Dr. Bruce Perry.[24] This is not meant to diminish the impact of trauma, but rather to help hold the whole story.

So, let's look at what's really going on in the aftermath of childhood adversity.

 Trauma is not being sure you have the resources to survive.

 Toxic stress and trauma set your nervous system up for a life of survival on your own. (Remember The Mistrust Cycle.)

 Trying to survive on your own can lead to some behavior that others don't like and that might not serve you well in the long run.

 Your Downstairs Brain needed to run the show, and...that's not the end of the story.

 Superheroes are born from adversity.

The larger premise of this book is not just that "it's a brain thing," but that brains can change! We are constantly forming new connections and pruning what we no longer need, a concept known as neuroplasticity. More than white-knuckling it through the school year, the seven keys featured in Part Two of this book will help you become a brain builder for your students (and maybe for yourself and your colleagues as well).

 The premise behind the term "post-traumatic wisdom" is that you can use your experiences to understand yourself and others more deeply. As Dr. Perry says, "You use your pain and transform it to power and help other people." *Are there any examples of this that you can think of from your life?*

HOPE FOR THE JOURNEY

Relationships are the agents of change,
and the most powerful therapy is human love.

– Bruce Perry, M.D., Ph.D.

Our brains tend to like easy answers and simple solutions. Appreciating neurodiversity, talking about trauma, and digging into the complexities of human development can activate those Downstairs Brain protectors! I spent a good chunk of my early career in Turtle mode, overwhelmed by the weight of the systemic injustice and generational trauma all around me. Maybe like me, your heart feels heavy and it's hard to think straight at times. Or perhaps your prickly Porcupine brain is sending thoughts like, "No one has time for this touchy-feely stuff. Get on with it, lady."

There were times I felt hopeless on this journey of coming alongside those who were struggling—big behaviors at home, destruction in the classroom, chaos into adulthood, and broken relationships everywhere! Learning what is *really* going on—and what we can do about it—has restored my hope. As we come to the end of Part One, let's recap these five foundational facts that will support you on this learning journey:

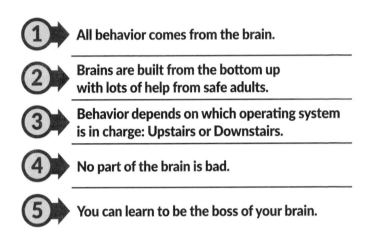

1 All behavior comes from the brain.

2 Brains are built from the bottom up with lots of help from safe adults.

3 Behavior depends on which operating system is in charge: Upstairs or Downstairs.

4 No part of the brain is bad.

5 You can learn to be the boss of your brain.

It is never too late to learn how to be the boss of your brain!

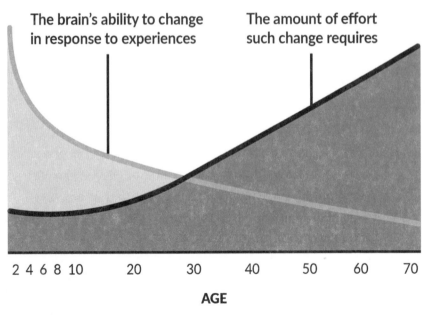

The brain's ability to change in response to experiences

The amount of effort such change requires

2 4 6 8 10   20   30   40   50   60   70

AGE

SOURCE: HTTPS://DEVELOPINGCHILD.HARVARD.EDU/SCIENCE/KEY-CONCEPTS/BRAIN-ARCHITECTURE/

It may become more difficult to create new habits as we get older, but humans have tremendous capacity for change. As Margaret Mead famously said, "Never doubt that a small group of thoughtful, committed citizens can change the world; indeed, it's the only thing that ever has." Let's do the work so we can help our students build their big, brave, beautiful, world-changing brains. The time to start is now!

> *"Never doubt that a small group of thoughtful, committed citizens can change the world; indeed, it's the only thing that ever has."*

 Dr. Perry emphasizes that trauma-informed practice involves both understanding trauma's impact and our responsibility to act accordingly. He calls us to ask ourselves—whether you are a teacher, counselor, or superintendent—*What do we do now?*

- *What is one thing you have learned about ACEs or PCEs that impacts your work?*

- *What thoughts and questions on this topic are still on your mind?*

There is hope. Keep reading. I'm excited to help you light up the learning brain—and maybe learn a few helpful things about your brain along the way!

KEY TAKEAWAYS

- Adverse Childhood Experiences, commonly called ACEs, impact the body and brain in ways that require compassionate understanding and support, not reactive punishments.

- Participating in community traditions and having at least two non-parent adults who take a genuine interest are just two of the Positive Childhood Experiences, or PCEs, that have been shown to protect against the negative impact of ACEs.

- Brains can change! This is important for you, your students, and all the adults who are part of your school community.

- Even in the face of adversity, toxic stress, and trauma, there is hope.

LOW-STRESS STARTING POINT

Build habits that support your Upstairs Brain.

Lisa Olivera, author of the fantastic book *Already Enough*, recommends making small shifts like these to nourish your brain and body.[25] Choose one (or create your own) and stick with it all week to help you shift from protection mode to connection mode.

Instead of this:	Try this:
Checking your phone first thing in the morning	Journal or stretch before reaching for your phone
Mindlessly checking your emails throughout the day	Check at times when you're able to read and respond
Having no plan for lunch or dinner and getting too hungry to think	Plan a few meals to ease stress and nourish your body
Waiting until you're exhausted to slow down and rest	Schedule in rest and recuperation regularly
Staying seated in the same spot throughout the day	Make it a point to get up and move your body regularly

PART TWO 2

KEYS TO UNLOCK STUDENT AND STAFF POTENTIAL

KEY ONE:
BECOME A BRAIN BUILDER

KEY TWO:
GET *ALL* THE SENSES INVOLVED

KEY THREE:
PLAY AND BE PLAYFUL

KEY FOUR:
BE CURIOUS

KEY FIVE:
CREATE A CULTURE OF SAFETY

KEY SIX:
SHARE THE POWER

KEY SEVEN:
LEAD WITH THE BRAIN IN MIND

BECOME A
BRAIN BUILDER

This is where hope lives for all of us,
in the unique adaptability of our brains.

– Oprah Winfrey, *What Happened to You?*

Brain anatomy impacts every aspect of human life. Want to increase learning opportunities, reduce negative behavior, and improve both staff and student morale? Become a brain builder!

EQUIP YOUR STAFF

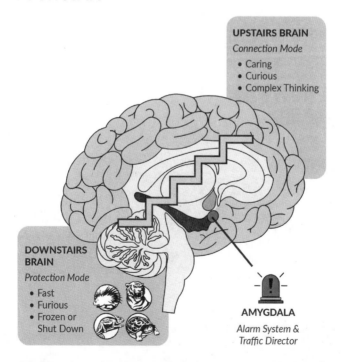

UPSTAIRS BRAIN
Connection Mode
- Caring
- Curious
- Complex Thinking

DOWNSTAIRS BRAIN
Protection Mode
- Fast
- Furious
- Frozen or Shut Down

AMYGDALA
*Alarm System &
Traffic Director*

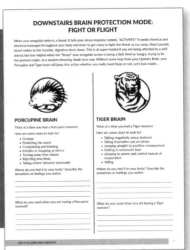

Please visit ncyi.org/lightupthelearningbrain to access the downloadable resources.

Enter the code below to unlock the resources.

LIGHT532

DOWNSTAIRS BRAIN PROTECTION MODE: FIGHT OR FLIGHT

When your amygdala detects a threat, it tells your stress response system, "ACTIVATE!" It sends chemical and electrical messages throughout your body and brain to get ready to fight the threat or run away. Heart pounds, blood rushes to the muscles, digestion shuts down. This is all super helpful if you are being attacked by a wild animal, but less helpful when the "threat" your amygdala senses is being a little fired or hungry, trying to fix the jammed copier, or a student throwing shade your way. Without some help from your Upstairs Brain, your Porcupine and Tiger brain will jump into action whether you really need them or not. Let's look inside...

PORCUPINE BRAIN

Think of a time you had a Porcupine moment.

Here are some clues to look for:
- Grumpy
- Predicting the worst
- Complaining and blaming
- Irritable or snapping at others
- Turning away from others
- Rejecting new ideas
- Taking others' behavior personally

Where do you feel it in your body? Describe the sensations or feelings you notice.

What do you need when you are having a Porcupine moment?

TIGER BRAIN

Think of a time you had a Tiger moment.

Here are some clues to look for:
- Taking negatively about students
- Taking frustration out on others
- Jumping straight to punitive consequences
- Getting in someone's face
- Jumping to power and control instead of cooperation
- Yelling

Where do you feel it in your body? Describe the sensations or feelings you notice.

What do you need when you are having a Tiger moment?

Before jumping into sharing this brainy goodness with their students, it is important that staff understand the brain-behavior connection more deeply. One of the most effective strategies I have found for getting started may surprise you.

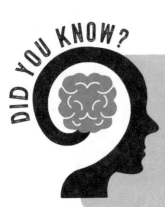

DID YOU KNOW?

Stories—like movies, books, oral storytelling, and even songs—activate a front-to-back connection in the brain called the Default Mode Network (DMN). Using stories helps us more fully integrate new information.

Stories soothe the amygdala alarm system and help the Upstairs Brain engage, so I wrote *Riley the Brave*, a brightly-colored picture book, to present this trauma-sensitive framework in story form. Images and metaphors also enhance learners' ability to understand and retain complex

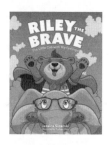

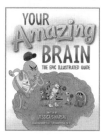

concepts, so I have created *Your Amazing Brain* with engaging visuals for ages 7 and up. While I will summarize the essentials in this chapter, I encourage you to read the books. I kept them short on purpose! Check them out from your local library or, better yet, stock your classroom or school library with a copy or two.

> "Wait! A picture book? I lead a staff of high school teachers who won't want anything to do with that!" Riley the Brave has been used with rowdy kids, teens, adults who have "seen it all," grumpy grandparents, incarcerated individuals, college students, and beyond. Your Amazing Brain makes the science even more tangible—in an engaging graphic novel style. If your staff is skeptical, try saying: "I know this is unconventional, but hang with me." You might even share that storytelling hits a different part of the brain than lecture alone, so you're doing their tired teacher brains a favor by introducing the topic this way.

Step One: Quick Review

Review 29:39–49:39 of the "It's a Brain Thing!" video available on my YouTube channel at bit.ly/BBactivity (case sensitive).[26] This will allow you to virtually sit in on a short class with me where we walk through the Downstairs Brain moments in a way you can use with your staff.

Step Two: Share Foundational Points

During professional development, a staff meeting, or within your learning community, review the following foundational points:

- The brain has two main operating systems: the Upstairs Brain and Downstairs Brain.
- Brains are built from the bottom up with lots of help from caring adults.
- Brains are diverse.
- All behavior comes from the brain. If you are trying to prevent or deal with "bad behavior," it is important to understand what is going on in the brain.

Step Three: Incorporate Stories and Visuals

"BRAINS: Journey to Resilience" is the best video I have seen for sharing complex ACEs and resilience research in a creative and strengths-based manner. Find it at 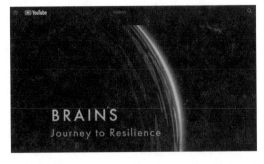 http://y2u.be/HJvDrT6N-mw. I also recommend reading sections of *Your Amazing Brain* and/or *Riley the Brave*, to highlight the following key concepts:

- We all have times when the "Act Without Thinking" team takes over. It's a brain thing!
- Everyone needs connection to safe adults (aka "safe big critters").
- Without a felt sense of safety, the brain prioritizes solo survival. Big feelings and defensive behaviors ("Downstairs

Brain moments") become the norm. It is not a weakness—it is quite courageous.

- Safety, connection, and care let us learn new ways to be brave. There is hope!

"I can't be everyone's safe person!!" No, it is not your job to be *the* safe big critter for all your students. If you are working with a student who has lots of Downstairs Brain behavior, though, it is important that you are sending emotional, physical, and relational messages of safety. Your brain will want to get defensive or reactive. Maybe you're bristling a little right now as you read this, feeling like I'm asking too much. After all, you became a teacher to teach! Unfortunately, for that mistrusting brain to learn what you are teaching, it needs to feel some safety. That's why I devoted a whole chapter to the topic of creating safety. Please know that I understand your concerns and will do my very best to address them as we continue this brain-based journey.

Step Four: Provide X-Ray Vision for the Downstairs Brain

Share the four Downstairs Brain characters with the group. Utilize teaching methods like "think/pair/share," taking turns reading aloud, or asking open-ended questions to encourage engagement. While these discussions may naturally turn toward student behavior, the next step will be to gently turn the conversation toward self-reflection. For example, "Yes, we have seen a lot of Porcupine moments in Cristina lately. When that happens, it's only natural that our Downstairs Brains kick in too! Let's look at how this plays out for *us* and see if that gives us any insight into what this means in the classroom."

Step Five: Reflection Activity

Lead a self-reflective discussion or quiet activity time about our own Downstairs Brain moments using the two-page guide in your downloadable resources. It may help to print a copy for each staff member or small group. Don't have time for all four "moments?" Get started with PORCUPINE and then ask the group to pick one more the next few times you gather.

- Use portions of the "It's a Brain Thing!" video if it is helpful for your group.

- Discuss each Downstairs Brain moment, paying attention to what sensations you feel (i.e. what clues your body gives you— tight shoulders, fuzzy thinking, upset stomach, heat up the back of the neck, etc.) and the needs that arise.

- Notice how the needs related to the same "moment" vary by person and situation. Encourage empathy within the group, noticing similarities and accepting differences.

- Downstairs Brain moments aren't bad! Everyone needs to Turtle sometimes, and that Tiger inside can really help us out in a pinch. We just need to get to know these powerful protectors so they don't feel like they have to take over all the time!

Remember, no one *is* a Tiger or Porcupine, but we all have those moments. The more we get to know our Downstairs Brain, the better chance we have of keeping some Upstairs Brain control during difficult situations.

Wrapping Up: Be Prepared for Downstairs Brain Reactions

If you get pushback, if you see some prickly Porcupine moments happening as you share this information, try saying something like:

- "Hey, I get it. You're here to teach and maybe this feels like fluffy stuff. If we don't want to get stuck in power struggles or *insert the problem of the day* it really helps to get to know our brains."

- "If this feels too personal, you don't have to share today. It is important for all of us to reflect. Please reach out later if you need some additional support."

If your own Downstairs Brain is kicking in you might find yourself not wanting to engage with the exercise or thinking, "Now I feel worse about myself. I'm not sure my Upstairs Brain is ever in charge!" Remember, if your Downstairs Brain is extra strong, it had a reason! Maybe you had some tough stuff early in life. Maybe you have been fighting against racism or other forms of bias much of your life. Maybe you were born with a "warrior" amygdala (anxiety) that really, really wants to keep you safe![27] The good news is—you can change your brain.

What is one thing you learned about yourself that you want to remember?

EMPOWER YOUR STUDENTS

Now let's take this brain-building know-how straight to those growing minds we all care so much about. This knowledge is essential if we want to help students become the bosses of their own brains. Find helpful visuals, language, and lesson ideas for each age group. Keep in mind, these ages/grades are just suggestions. Here and throughout this book, please use the strategies that you are drawn to or that you think will resonate with your students. The rest of this book will build on these foundational concepts, providing additional tools for weaving this brain-boosting framework into your routine.

> "Isn't this the counselor's job? I don't have time to teach about the brain!" Perhaps your school or district will set things up in a way that ensures that the counselor, SEL specialist, or other supportive person is tackling the first introduction of these concepts, but your involvement will benefit you and your students! As you will continue to see throughout this book, spending a little time up front, changing a few habits, and learning some new language will save you time! And you'll probably enjoy your job more along the way. It may not be what you learned in school – it's not what I learned either – but I have seen first-hand how using these brain-based keys changes lives. I promise it will be time well spent.

GRADES PREK-2

Use the following language and visuals to teach your students about their brains. For your youngest students, keep your explanation simpler. Try introducing just one concept per week, building up to understanding more of the downstairs characters over time.

Step One: House Model of the Brain

"Did you know we have two main parts of our brain, and only ONE can be in charge at a time? The Upstairs Brain helps us play, learn, and have fun with others. It also helps us solve problems and deal with the big feelings that we all have! The Downstairs Brain can help us stay safe in tough situations, but it also gets us in trouble! When we feel upset or unsafe, our Turtle and Porcupine powers try to take over."

Step Two: Your Amygdala Alarm

"Are you ready to learn a funny word? There is a special part of your Downstairs Brain called the amygdala [uh-MIG-duh-luh], which acts like an alarm system and traffic director. It instantly decides if the messages coming into your brain from your senses are safe enough for your Upstairs Brain to run things, or... DANGER! DANGER! Your Downstairs Brain takes over, acting without thinking. The amygdala sends one of your animal superpowers in to save the day!"

Step Three: Introduce the Downstairs Brain Characters

"Big feelings can be confusing for the amygdala. Sometimes your amygdala sends in a grumpy, prickly Downstairs Brain power like a Porcupine when we don't need the help. That's what Riley the Brave calls 'Having a Porcupine moment.'"

I designed the books in the series *Riley the Brave's Adventures* to make it easier to introduce these complicated concepts. Use puppets or stuffed animals to bring these Downstairs Brain protectors to life. With young students, you may want to stick with just the Tiger and Turtle for a while. In addition to the printable activity available in the downloads for this book, try playing out scenes, using silly voices and stuffed animals or puppets, and looking for these Downstairs Brain moments in other stories you read together.

Step Four: Make the Brain-Body Connection

"Your brain is connected to your body. Okay, that might seem obvious, but it's an important part of this. We have to notice the messages our bodies are sending to understand which part of the brain is in charge. Plus, we can use our bodies to get that powerful Upstairs Brain back in charge."

Step Five: Becoming the Boss of Your Brain

"There are times we need our Downstairs Brain powers. Sometimes, though, they get extra protective, and we end up hurting ourselves or others. Getting to know your brain and body better will help you climb out of those Turtle and Porcupine moments and get your Upstairs Brain back in control." Find this 2-page activity in your downloadable resources to expand on these lessons.

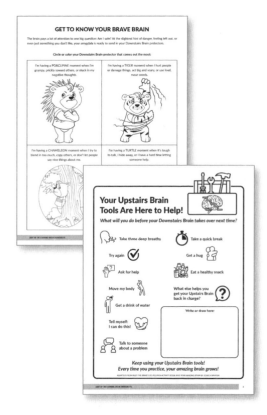

GRADES 3-5

This guide will help you teach your students about their amazing brains. Make this part of your morning meeting, advisory, or designated time for social emotional learning. Wherever you fit it in, I promise it will be time well spent.

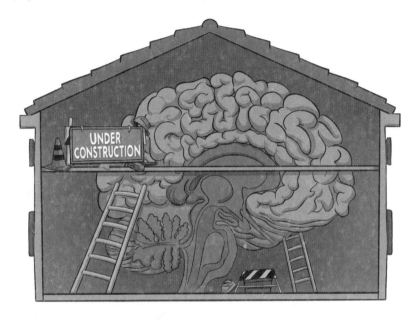

Step One: House Model of the Brain

"Did you know your brain has stairs? Okay, not really, but your brain is a lot like a two-story house that is under construction."

The Downstairs Brain is ready to go at birth. It's in charge of important things like breathing and making our hearts beat. It is also the home of the limbic [LIM-bik] system, which is where our feelings and memories live. The Downstairs Brain helps keep us alive, but it acts without thinking even when survival isn't on the line. Over time, construction happens on the more advanced, upper part of the brain.

The Upstairs Brain is the large, wrinkly outer portion of the brain, which is technically known as the cerebral [ser-EE-bruhl] cortex. It lets you do soooooo many important things, like play, learn, have fun, be creative, solve problems, and more! Because the Upstairs Brain thinks before acting, it can help us deal with the big feelings that come from the Downstairs Brain.

The Amygdala [uh-MIG-duh-luh] is a small part of the Downstairs Brain that acts like an alarm system and traffic director. In milliseconds, it decides if the messages being delivered by your senses are safe enough for your Upstairs Brain to run things, or... DANGER! DANGER! Your Downstairs Brain takes over, acting without thinking.

Step Two: Introduce the Downstairs Brain Characters

"The brain pays a lot of attention to one big question: Am I safe? At the slightest hint of danger, feeling left out, or even just something you don't like, your amygdala is ready to send in your Downstairs Brain protectors." Find this one-page printable in full color in the digital downloads that accompany this book.

Step Three: Make the Brain-Body Connection

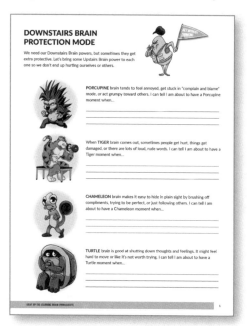

"Your brain is connected to your body. Okay, that might seem obvious, but it's an important part of this. We have to notice the messages our bodies are sending to understand which part of the brain is in charge. Plus, we can use our bodies to get that powerful Upstairs Brain back in charge."

Use this one-page reproducible to spark conversation about these four popular characters from the "Act Without Thinking" team and the clues we get from our bodies that they are taking over.

Step Four: You Can Be the Boss of Your Brain!

Our brains work best when messages are flowing smoothly between both teams. Here's a 3-step plan that can help us strengthen the staircase of our minds. Try practicing with an example from a story you recently read or some other fictional situation. You might also share that you as an adult are also learning to be the boss of your brain, and

when your Tiger brain says, "That's it. Take away recess for a week," you have to take a breath, get some help from your curious, problem-solving Upstairs Brain, and then choose a wise solution.

Keep the learning going! The book *Your Amazing Brain* was designed to make it easier to share these complicated concepts with upper elementary students and beyond. In it, you will find:

- Brain cell and nervous system basics
- Eight senses and where the brain gets its information
- House and hand models of the brain with the two brain teams explained
- Strategies for helping your Upstairs Brain run the show
- Fun and useful facts about the brain with some additional brain boosting know-how
- A guide for grown-ups
- Additional activities

GRADES 6-12

Sometimes getting started is the hardest part. Here are a few ideas to choose from. Remember, this book is meant to be written in and customized for *you*, so jot some notes or make a plan right in the margins!

- Try sparking curiosity about the brain with one of the puzzles at www.brainfacts.org/for-educators.
- Anyone else remember the egg-in-the-frying-pan ad from the '80s?[28] "This is your brain. This is your brain on drugs. Any questions?" I remember seeing it on television as a kid, long before it was a viral meme-generator, and I had lots of questions. Show your students that you're not here to

dumb things down. Maybe start with that video and let your students know that you are open to questions about the brain. You won't know all the answers, and that's okay!

- Start with a little honesty. You might say, "I just learned something interesting that I want to share with you. I know this isn't what we usually talk about, but it's pretty cool." Put your own personality and wording into it! Students appreciate knowing their teachers are human.

Once you've settled their amygdalas a bit and sparked some Upstairs Brain curiosity, share some brain science with your students. After lots of consultation with teachers and mental health professionals—and days of laboring over how much information to provide—I created the following printable resources to help you on your brainy journey.

Feel free to flip back to previous sections as you decide what would be most meaningful for your specific group of students. Some of the same strategies used with staff or with grades 3-5 can be helpful for this age group as well. Then, keep the learning going all year by referencing the Upstairs and Downstairs Brain frequently. And because teens are the experts on themselves, I ran these lesson ideas by my seventh and ninth graders. Here is their advice:

- **Be curious. Don't act like you know everything. Kids won't like that.**

- **Expect belligerence.** To which I said, "Of course, it's the developmental stage teens are in." That's when they said, "Don't tell kids about the developmental stage they are in." See first bullet point. 😉

- **When the snide comments come, try using a little playfulness to manage them.** Okay, they didn't say it just like that, but the examples they gave showed teachers not taking it personally and using humor to diffuse the situation. More on that when we get to Key Three.

- **Explain the details. Don't be too cutesy. Tell us the science. We want to know.** Remember, you won't know all the answers, and that is okay! You don't have to be the expert, just a trusted companion on the learning journey.

FOR THE ADULTS AT HOME

The previous sections contain simple one-page explanations and lots of visuals to make it easy to share this information with parents and caregivers. Include whichever tool you used with a brief note like this:

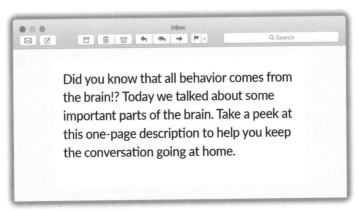

> Did you know that all behavior comes from the brain!? Today we talked about some important parts of the brain. Take a peek at this one-page description to help you keep the conversation going at home.

Find additional resources to support families
at www.JessicaSinarski.com.

THE BUILDING BLOCKS FOR LEARNING

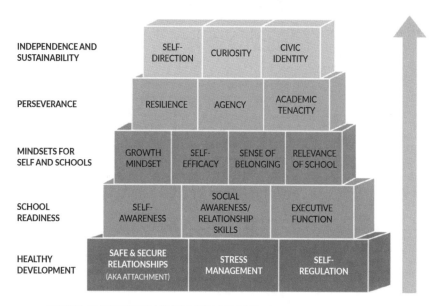

INDEPENDENCE AND SUSTAINABILITY	SELF-DIRECTION	CURIOSITY	CIVIC IDENTITY
PERSEVERANCE	RESILIENCE	AGENCY	ACADEMIC TENACITY
MINDSETS FOR SELF AND SCHOOLS	GROWTH MINDSET / SELF-EFFICACY	SENSE OF BELONGING	RELEVANCE OF SCHOOL
SCHOOL READINESS	SELF-AWARENESS	SOCIAL AWARENESS/ RELATIONSHIP SKILLS	EXECUTIVE FUNCTION
HEALTHY DEVELOPMENT	SAFE & SECURE RELATIONSHIPS (AKA ATTACHMENT)	STRESS MANAGEMENT	SELF-REGULATION

SOURCE: ADAPTED FROM "BUILDING BLOCKS FOR LEARNING: A FRAMEWORK FOR COMPREHENSIVE STUDENT DEVELOPMENT" BY TURNAROUND FOR CHILDREN[29]

Now that you are a little more familiar with the brain, let's look at how the *learning* brain, specifically, is built. Drawing from research across multiple fields, Drs. K. Brooke Stafford-Brizard and Pamela Cantor have outlined the skills and mindsets that are strongly correlated to, and may even predict, academic achievement. Each block builds on those below, and it all begins with the development of a healthy attachment system (i.e. safe and secure relationships), stress management skills, and the capacity for self-regulation.[30]

SAFE & SECURE RELATIONSHIPS (AKA ATTACHMENT)

A deep and enduring emotional bond that connects one person to another across time and space.

STRESS MANAGEMENT

Constantly changing cognitive and behavioral efforts to manage specific external and/or internal demands that are appraised as taxing or exceeding the resources of the person.

SELF-REGULATION

Regulation of attention, emotion, and executive functions for the purposes of goal-directed actions.

Brains are built from the bottom up, and that "construction" is an intensely relational experience. You can do all the decorating you want upstairs, but those growth mindset posters won't keep the foundation from cracking. Tending to these core building blocks is a critical part of strengthening the "staircase of the brain," those neural connections that help us find our way out of defense mode to light up the learning brain.

Because the foundational building blocks are forged in the context of relationship, it's easy to "blame the parents" when you are working with a student who is struggling. There are so many reasons a child may struggle with any one of these skills, mindsets, or traits, but I have never seen shame and blame lead to positive solutions. Keep reading for more ideas on how you can be a brain builder, even in difficult circumstances.

KEY TAKEAWAYS

- Teaching staff and students a few brain essentials doesn't have to be complicated:

  - There are two main operating systems in the brain: the Upstairs Brain and Downstairs Brain.

  - We all have times when the amygdala sends a false alarm and the "Act Without Thinking" parts of our brain take over, creating Tiger, Turtle, Porcupine, and Chameleon moments.

  - Understanding how the brain works helps reduce shame and blame so that we can have our Upstairs Brains run the show more and more.

- Sometimes getting started is the hardest part. After all, the brain struggles with change, even if it has a positive result.

- Tools in this chapter will help you use brain-based language as you check in with yourself, students, and the whole school community. For example, ask yourself, "What part of my brain is in charge? Where is this student/staff member in their brain?"

- Safe and secure relationships, stress management, and self-regulation form the bedrock for future academic success. Tending to these areas will help you light up the learning brain.

LOW-STRESS STARTING POINT

When you want to dole out consequences (a clue that your Downstairs Brain is kicking into action), try saying it out loud.

- "I want to take away recess. I am choosing to be patient. I need quiet in 10, 9, 8..."

- "I'm having a hard time staying in my Upstairs Brain when I see *insert frustrating behavior*. Let's pause and regroup."

- "Woah. I think there's a blackout in our Upstairs Brains! Let's take a quick stretch break and see if we can get the lights back on."

- CLAP—CLAP—CLAP, CLAP, CLAP *Wait for response and repeat.* "Things are feeling out of control in here. Let's cool out and try *insert specific instruction* again."

Remember to make these scripts your own. As long as the words are coming from your Upstairs Brain, your personality, style, and strengths will make these brain-building strategies even more powerful for you and your students.

GET *ALL* THE SENSES INVOLVED

*The senses are gateways to the intelligence.
There is nothing in the intelligence which did not
first pass through the senses.*

- Aristotle

Here is the magic of understanding our senses. Joe (real person but not his real name) was diagnosed with Generalized Anxiety Disorder and was in counseling by age six. Over the next few years, various psychologists and therapists taught him and his parents every tool they had to help calm his anxiety and reduce his meltdowns. But nothing changed. Actually, things got worse.

This creative, compassionate kid was plagued by stress and school challenges. Despite the support of highly invested parents, teachers, and mental health professionals, his bizarre behavior disrupted class time, and meltdowns continued. One afternoon, sitting across from yet another new therapist, Joe told his mom that he didn't want to keep living if this was how life would be. He was only nine years old.

His parents reached out to me, understandably heartbroken and distraught. As they talked about his "symptoms," my heart broke too. It seemed clear that his brain was in survival mode, and his senses were all out of whack. His Downstairs Brain was running the show!

Unfortunately, all the tools he had been given by well-intentioned professionals required Upstairs Brain powers that he couldn't access! Remember, only one operating system can be in charge at a time. Joe had been living in a nearly constant state of fight, flight, or freeze. Being told to "use a coping skill" was just heaping on more feelings of failure, brokenness, and shame. Joe's distressing thoughts and behavior were coming from distressed senses sending confusing signals to his little brain.

JOE'S DISTRESSING THOUGHTS AND BEHAVIOR WERE COMING FROM DISTRESSED SENSES.

To unlock Joe's potential, we needed to get *all* the senses involved.

"Wait! Are you saying that we can't tell students to use their coping skills?" Coping skills can be incredibly helpful, but we must think about what part of the brain is in charge both when we are asking and when that particular strategy is useful. If we are asking a brain in full Turtle or Tiger mode to use a rational, language-based skill, it is not going to go well. The same is true for us as adults. Keep reading for lots more strategies that will reach distressed brains.

THE BRAIN→BEHAVIOR→SENSES CONNECTION

Are you working with older students? Don't skip this chapter! While sensory-rich learning is especially important in the early years, I will show you how harnessing the power of the senses benefits tweens, teens, and adults as well.

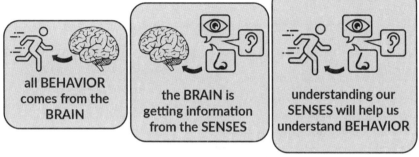

all BEHAVIOR comes from the BRAIN

the BRAIN is getting information from the SENSES

understanding our SENSES will help us understand BEHAVIOR

SOURCE: JESSICA SINARSKI

Everything we feel, think, say, and do is related to the information coming in through our senses, and we have more than you might think. Our senses help us enjoy life, but when they are confused or overwhelmed, they get extra protective! There is a wide range of "typical" sensory preferences, for example, the weight of blanket or type of fabric you like, certain smells or sounds that bother you, etc. In contrast, for people with sensory processing difficulties, every aspect of life is impacted by a swirl of too much and too little information coming into the brain. Here's what that might look like in your students:

Can't organize their desks		Crave organization in everything
Love messy play - bring on the sand, glue, mud, and glitter		Can't stand anything on their hands
Have trouble sitting up straight		Can climb, jump, and crash around without getting hurt
Passive, quiet, and withdrawn		Hyperactive, loud, and in everyone's space
Love noises, smells, and bright lights		Can't stand most smells, sounds, or visual clutter

Since there are so many combinations of how our senses might interact with each other, sensory processing challenges often go undetected. This chapter will help you harness the power of the senses for your whole school community, including both neurotypical and neurodivergent students.

DID YOU KNOW?

Sensory processing impacts everyone, not just the autistic community. Research shows that Sensory Processing Disorder (SPD) can occur without any other neurodivergence, such as being autistic, and often co-occurs with other learning differences and mental health diagnoses.[31] Please refer to the "Brains are Diverse" section on page 26 for additional information about diagnosis and neurodivergence.

WE HAVE ~~FIVE~~ EIGHT SENSES

You have heard about sight, hearing, smell, taste, and touch, but did you know that humans have *three more senses*? It was a surprise to me too when I first learned about proprioception, interoception, and the vestibular system. It was even more surprising to learn how vital these senses are to feeling safe and healthy in our daily lives.

LEARN MORE ABOUT ALL EIGHT SENSES IN
RILEY THE BRAVE'S SENSATIONAL SENSES BY JESSICA SINARSKI,
ILLUSTRATED BY ZACHARY KLINE.

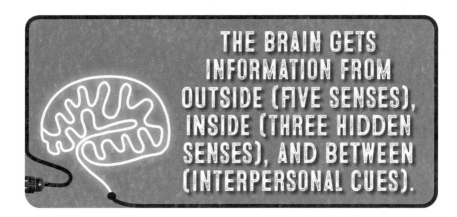

THE BRAIN GETS INFORMATION FROM OUTSIDE (FIVE SENSES), INSIDE (THREE HIDDEN SENSES), AND BETWEEN (INTERPERSONAL CUES).

Remember, the brain gets information from OUTSIDE (five senses), INSIDE (three hidden senses), and BETWEEN (interpersonal cues). Let's learn a little more about those hidden senses that impact behavior!

Proprioception

Proprioception is your sense of self in space. It comes into your brain from receptors in the muscles and joints all over your body and plays a big role in planning our movements and what we often think of as "self-control." Proprioception is an incredibly helpful sense to understand, especially for preschool and elementary students, who naturally need more of this grounding, regulating input. Without the right amount of proprioceptive input, it is difficult to keep my hands to myself, write (a surprisingly complicated physical activity), carry on a conversation, or even sit still! Seems like something we should be paying attention to if we want to light up the learning brain!

A child who needs more proprioceptive input may:

- Play rough with others
- Bump into people and things
- Climb, crawl, or jump everywhere they can

- Fidget, kick the desk, or have difficulty sitting still

- Seem agitated or distracted during sedentary tasks

The Vestibular System \ Sense of Balance

This important sense begins its work *in utero*. It is constantly detecting the head's position through tiny receptors in the inner ear, preventing injury by keeping the head upright. With its location so close to the brainstem and emotional center of the brain, the vestibular system is a key player in feeling safe and in control. Our brains need lots of experiences of rocking, rolling, swinging, and crawling to nourish this foundational system.

Interoception

This sense comes from the nerves in our organs and gives us lots of critical information for everyday life, like "Hey, you're hungry," and "Ow, don't touch that." It also helps us feel our emotions, like the tightness you might notice in your chest when you feel anxious or the heat up the back of your neck when you are angry. Environments and activities that help kids feel safe and in control create space for increased attention to those internal messages. Making connections out loud about your own sensations is excellent modeling for kids who might struggle with the self-reflection and mindfulness that nurture this important sense.

PROPRIOCEPTION: THE SECRET SYSTEM FOR FEELING SAFE AND IN CONTROL

My brilliant little 4-year-old son was asked to draw a house at preschool and burst into tears. Bursting into tears was a common occurrence for him, as was picky eating, banging into things, difficulty transitioning from one task to the next, slouching posture, and what I came to realize were a whole host of sensory red flags.

Just as I was learning about how the senses were impacting the kids and families I was working with, sensory processing got very personal. My son would crash his knees into the hardwood floor, he was constantly in motion, chewing on everything, and, despite his sweet disposition, he seemed agitated and stressed much of the time. How did all this relate to not being able to draw a house at preschool? My eyes were about to be opened to the complexities of the senses, and one system in particular that needed a lot more input: pro-pree-oh-SEP-shun.

While each of the hidden senses is important in different ways, a cursory understanding of proprioception can yield quick results in the school setting. Skeptical? So was I! I remember sitting in the occupational therapist's office saying, "You're telling me that bouncing on a trampoline will help my child have fewer meltdowns? What does core strength have to do with handwriting?" But the more I learned, the more it made sense (no pun intended). We started doing "steam rollers" along his back and big "super slams" before bed. It was physical and full of laughter, just what you would think would amp up a little kid. Instead, he would sigh and say, "Ahhhh. Now I'm ready for sleeps." Building his core strength helped him have the postural stability he needed to write, and chewing gum *still* helps him focus.

DID YOU KNOW?

The jumping, crashing, squishing, squeezing, pushing, and pulling that nourish this sense tend to be enjoyable and regulating for most kids.

I have seen this same journey play out with countless kids since, like Joe from the beginning of this chapter. Before getting some proprioceptive tools in his toolbox, Joe was missing whole afternoons of instruction time. His teacher said, "When he's upset, he's gone. Nothing we do can get him

back." They tried all the coping strategies they knew, but they weren't harnessing the power of the senses. Now Joe does a few minutes of deep muscle work a couple times each day. His stress management includes a little pushing, pulling, bike pedaling, jumping, or crab walks, which enables him to become "learning-ready," rather than losing hours of instruction and then feeling lost with assignments. It made it easier for the teacher to teach. It helped the other students avoid losing class time. Are you seeing the power of understanding our sensational senses?

Because proprioceptive input tends to be regulating for everyone and is critically important for our preschool and elementary students, here are a few options to incorporate for the whole class or any student who needs a little extra "prope."

- Jump to your spot in line then stretch up high. Once you're all in line with hands high, clap your hands on the sides of your thighs and let them rest there or in your pockets.

- During circle time, make french-fry fingers in your lap. Kids who need a little movement can push and pull on their own hands.

- Do some wall push-ups between subjects—remember to make it playful!

- Jump challenge! Can you jump 10 times in a row on the same spot? How about 20? Get the blood flowing and then take a big, deep breath in, and breathe out as slowly as you can as you sit down in your seat.

- Take a 2-minute clapping break when energy is lagging after lunch. Get it started with the pattern: LAP, CLAP, CROSS, CLAP. Then try having a couple students offer a pattern to follow.

- Since we have muscles and joints in our mouths, chewing gum gives the proprioceptive system a boost! Try using this bubblegum club form to mindfully incorporate gum chewing in the younger grades.

- After lunch, have young students give themselves a big hug or do a few jumping jacks. For older students, maybe try a plank pose or ask for their suggestions of how to get blood flowing to the brain again.

- Engage energetic children in heavy muscle work, such as moving desks or carrying a heavy box of books to another teacher.

As you get to know this powerful sense, you will begin to see just how often the kids in your life are craving proprioceptive input.

"But my students will get too rowdy!" You may need to co-regulate back to that "just right" spot after doing some of these activities, especially with younger students. Try slowing your claps down together or pretending to move slowly through thick honey to get back to their seats. End your activity with a big, deep, full body breath with a long exhale as they get back to work. All these activities also build their self-regulation muscles, which sounds like a win-win to me!

THE SENSES AND SELF-REGULATION

Early life is meant to be a sensory-rich time. Babies are bounced, patted, snuggled, and rocked to the sweet sound of lullabies. Even sucking on a binkie and being swaddled for sleep help provide the diverse sensations that the infant's brain and body need.

For most parents, it takes some time to figure out the right combination of soothing moves to help their baby settle. Plus, it seems like as soon as you figure out something that works, it changes, forcing you to tune in to your baby's needs again and try something different to soothe your fussy little one. This is part of the co-regulation process that precedes self-regulation.

The grown-up brings their calm and curious self to help the baby with whatever is upsetting them, whether it is a wet diaper, feeling hungry or cold, or needing help falling asleep. Parents and caregivers essentially become sensory detectives without realizing it, and all their hard work helps that little brain and body make vital connections that eventually lead to the ability to ask for what they need instead of wailing about it.

Fast forward to your classroom, break room, or district office, and the senses are still actively impacting behavior. Your sensory systems are sending eleven million bits of information to your brain every second![32] Even though we are only conscious of, at most, 40-50 of those bits, it is easy to see how the brain gets flooded. When overwhelmed, the brain tends to produce some mixed-up feelings and frustrating behaviors, those Downstairs Brain moments we have been talking about.

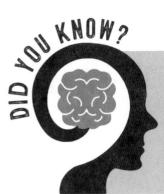

DID YOU KNOW?

Our sensory systems are sending eleven million bits of information to the brain every second!

When children do not behave as we expect them to, it is often because they can't... yet. Fortunately, that is not the end of the story. When we help children understand what their senses need, we are literally helping them grow their brains, increasing their capacity to "feel and deal" instead of flipping into Tiger brain or curling up in their Turtle shells. If you have a student who struggles with self-regulation, check in with the senses!

WHEN WE HELP STUDENTS UNDERSTAND WHAT THEIR SENSES NEED, WE ARE LITERALLY HELPING THEM GROW THEIR BRAINS.

THE SENSES GO TO SCHOOL

We all bring all our senses to school with us every day. Let's normalize it! For example, my sense of hearing is pretty sensitive in general. It means that I feel music in an intense, soul-stirring way, but it also means my boisterous family sometimes gives me a headache just by being themselves. There are times when I ask them to be quieter, and there are times it works best for all of us for me to wear a loose pair of earplugs. I also know that the crinkling of a plastic water bottle feels like a physical assault. If I am in a classroom full of crinkles and squeaks and noises galore, it's only a matter of time before my Tiger brain comes out unless we get on the same team. Sharing this with students might sound like:

- "Oooh, that sound doesn't work for me. Can you help me out and put it away?"

- *With a little playfulness*: "Aah! That sound feels like a hammer on my brain. Let's put the water bottle(s) away. Otherwise, my Tiger brain might want to swipe it!"

- "We are a team, and crinkling water bottles throw off this team member," as you raise your hand. "Let's not do it."

- "So, water bottles are a thing for me. Those flimsy plastic ones just kill my head. What are your pet peeves? Any sounds that bug you? How can we work together so we don't all end up with a headache at the end of the day?"

At the beginning of the school year or whenever you have shared a bit about the senses, have small group discussions or a reflective assignment about what each student notices in their own sensory preferences. Emphasize that you all must be a team in the classroom. In addition to helping students build their sensory toolbox, you can use this information to inform your lessons.

- Do you work better with music or quiet?

- What else helps you focus?

- What is distracting in our classroom environment?

- How can you tell if you need to move your body?

Be sure to check back in on how your plans are working for everyone. A white noise machine, which some students might find helpful, could be problematic for others. I was visiting my sister and her new baby, and one of her favorite settings on the sound machine was *super* annoying to me. She had other favorite settings, so she changed it, and I felt an immediate sense of relief. The same sound that was enjoyable to her was emotionally and physically painful to me! How often does this happen in the school setting without us realizing it? It is impossible to discipline, consequence, or punish a child (or adult) into healthy sensory processing! Instead, let's normalize understanding our senses.

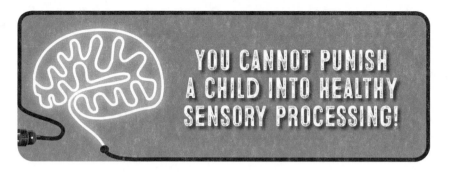

YOU CANNOT PUNISH A CHILD INTO HEALTHY SENSORY PROCESSING!

CREATE A SENSORY-FRIENDLY SCHOOL SETTING

In addition to suggestions throughout this chapter, this section offers strategies that tend to be helpful for all of our sensational senses.

- **Use gentle lighting.** Along with the benefits visually, the buzz of fluorescent lights may be an irritant under the surface for students and staff alike.

- **Reduce distracting noises.** Put tennis balls on chair legs or fabric on the walls.

- **Prioritize recess.** Don't take it away. Find ways to get outside more! Instead of a movie in class, how about extra time on the playground or heading outside for a walk?

- **Take brain breaks regularly.** Incorporate physical activity to support the hidden senses. Find more ideas at www.theOTtoolbox.com/brain-breaks.

- **Provide sensory-rich experiences to help learning "stick."** Go for hands-on experiences over worksheets and screens when possible. This is especially important for the younger grades, those with trauma histories, and many neurodiverse students.

- **Provide visual schedules and prompts.** Whenever you get more than one sense involved in instruction and expectations, you increase the likelihood that students with varied learning styles and sensory needs will be successful.

- Use a visual timer or interchangeable prompts on the board. A strong magnet can hold a sheet protector full of the prompts you use regularly.

- Get down to a student's level when trying to get attention. A gentle hand on the shoulder or other safe touch can be especially helpful for kids with explorer brains who might need a little extra support to go with the group plan.

- Emphasize the routine or pattern of things with physical gestures, miming what is expected or creating fun physical cues to help students remember.

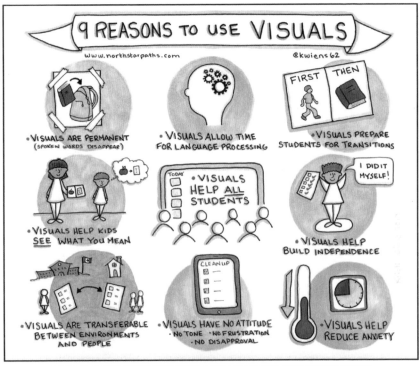

SOURCE: HTTPS://NORTHSTARPATHS.COM/GRAPHICS-FREE-DOWNLOADS/

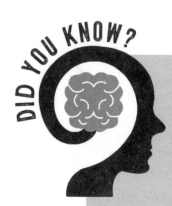

Research supports the benefits of getting the senses involved in learning.[33] For early readers, try using a small plastic "phone" to let them hear themselves reading aloud. Be sure to give clear instructions with visual cues about how LOUD their voices should be as they read. If you practice the "just right volume" playfully together before you dismiss them to their task, you help them strengthen their self-regulation skills!

TRAUMA AND THE SENSES

There are whole books on each of the sensory systems we have discussed in this chapter and the many ways they try to keep us safe. Adding a trauma-sensitive lens further complicates things, since the brain processes emotionally charged or life-threatening experiences in a primal, sensory way. Smell, for example, has a rapid path to the emotional center of the brain. This might lead to warm feelings when the smell of your grandmother's house lingers on your sweater after visiting or you catch the scent of your partner's cologne. It can have disastrous consequences as well because sensory information first impacts emotions on a subconscious level (in the Downstairs Brain).

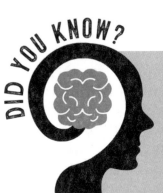

DID YOU KNOW?

Children who had stressful experiences early in life, such as foster care, medical trauma, or other big disruptions, commonly struggle with sensory processing difficulties. In fact, almost everyone with a trauma history benefits from some help making sense of their sensational senses.

In *What Happened to You?*, Dr. Bruce Perry shares a story of a student who had many difficult life experiences that impacted his behavior in school.[34] He was showing tremendous improvement when, seemingly out of nowhere, he began having big Tiger moments toward a teacher. In his observations, Dr. Perry couldn't see anything triggering happening in their interactions. The only pattern was that when this particular teacher got close, the boy would lose all Upstairs Brain function. Rage took over, even as the teacher was using all the brain-based strategies he knew! What was causing this huge negative reaction? The teacher was wearing the same deodorant the boy's abusive parent had worn.

There is much in the chapters ahead about how we can be curious and partner with our school and wider community to bring out the best in both students and staff. In the midst of those noble goals, we must remember that all behavior comes from the brain, and the brain is getting its information from...say it with me: OUTSIDE (five senses), INSIDE (three hidden senses) & BETWEEN (interpersonal cues).

KEY TAKEAWAYS

- Confused or overwhelmed senses send the brain into protection mode.

- The brain processes lots of information from our three hidden senses:

  - Proprioception (pressure, impact, and weight) coming from our muscles and joints

  - Vestibular (movement and balance) coming from the inner ear

  - Interoception (basic needs and internal monitoring) coming from the skin and internal organs

- When we help students understand what their senses need, we literally help them grow their brains.

- You can support the senses by increasing opportunities for sensory-rich instruction and learning while reducing distracting lights and noises in the classroom.

- Trauma and the senses are intimately linked, and sometimes the most unexpected sensory input can trigger Downstairs Brain protection mode.

LOW-STRESS STARTING POINT

When in doubt, "Go prope!"

If your class is a hot mess, take a brain break with proprioceptive input. Better yet, try it before the class falls apart! Do something rhythmic like a clapping game, a quick walk, or a group stretch. As you do it more regularly, let students take turns choosing a strategy to nourish their sensational senses.

PLAY AND BE PLAYFUL

Play is fundamentally important for learning 21st century skills, such as problem solving, collaboration, and creativity.

– American Academy of Pediatrics (AAP)

Play is a learning necessity, not a luxury. Admin, hear me out on the science. The above quote is from a clinical report provided by the American Academy of Pediatrics (AAP) detailing "additional evidence of the critical importance of play in facilitating parent engagement; promoting safe, stable, and nurturing relationships; encouraging the development of numerous competencies, including executive functioning skills; and improving life course trajectories."[35]

Promoting safe, stable, and nurturing relationships? Since safe and secure relationships are the cornerstone of learning, it sounds like play is something we should pay attention to!

Development of executive functioning skills? Yes, we want our students (and staff) to become better at planning, organizing, and following through!

Improving life course trajectories? Um...yes, please.

Teachers, leaders, support staff: this is not a request for you to fit one more thing into your day. The pages ahead will help you weave play and playfulness into what you are already doing to make your job easier *and* light up the learning brain in your students.

According to a Harvard study of adult development that has been going on for 85 years and counting, strong relationships keep us healthier and happier. "The one thing that continuously demonstrates its broad and enduring importance is good relationships."[36]

PLAY, CONNECTION, AND SENSING SAFETY

There's a reason that big corporations spend millions on ice breakers, obstacle courses, egg drop challenges, and other seemingly silly team-building events.

HUMANS WORK BETTER WHEN WE FEEL SAFE AND SECURE WITH OTHERS.

Play is a power tool for building connection and a sense of safety. This is essential for creating a positive school culture. Lighting up the learning brain requires a sense of connection among students, between students and teachers, and even among staff. Incorporate these potent relationship building tools into the beginning of the school year, staff meetings, and beyond.

SAFE & SECURE RELATIONSHIPS (AKA ATTACHMENT)

Doodle Board[37] (GR K-12, Staff)

Use a spare marker board as a doodle board. As students enter the classroom, or staff enter the meeting, they can take a minute to add their doodle to the board. This moment of levity provides a mental reset, gives a little spark of joy, and helps students or staff bond.

SOURCE: DR. RACHEL CULLEN @RACHCULLPHD ON INSTAGRAM

Write a daily, weekly, or monthly prompt, such as:

- Doodle something that makes you happy
- Doodle your favorite animal
- Doodle your favorite sport
- Doodle your dream job

Toss It! (GR 3-12, Staff)

This is a great check-in at the beginning of the school year and could easily be adapted for a mid-year check-in. Instructions:

1. Have participants tear a piece of paper into three pieces.

2. On the first paper, draw a line across the page. On that line, write a word or two to describe your school experience last year. Exchange with someone nearby and discuss.

3. On the second paper, write a plus (+) sign and one thing you are looking forward to this year. Exchange with someone across the room and discuss.

4. On the third paper, draw a question mark and write down something you are nervous or worried about this year or a question you have for me.

5. Pass all the papers forward or make it more playful by offering the chance to crumple all three papers and toss them your direction. See how many you can catch!

Not only is this a fun ice breaker, but it also gives you valuable data points about your school community. This is an important part of humanizing your data, one of eight critical reframes outlined in *Hacking Deficit Thinking*.[38] Authors McClure and Reed remind readers that this type of in-the-moment data helps us identify what's *right* in our students and schools rather than focusing only on what's *wrong*.

Let's Shake on It! (GR K-12)

Pair up and invent a fun handshake. Get creative and include fist or elbow bumps, dance moves, foot taps, high fives, and/or hand signals.

DID YOU KNOW?

A simple pat on the back communicates to the amygdala faster than spoken word.[39]

Let Gratitude Soar[40] (GR 4-12)

This is a fun gratitude activity that can be used in times of transition or any time your group needs a creative, uplifting boost.

1. Using a blank piece of paper, show students how to fold a paper airplane or have those in the group who know how team up with those who don't. Give them time to come up with new designs, test out their plane, or teach each other fun new ways to build.

2. Ask them to sit and reflect on something they are grateful for that can be anonymously shared with the class. Have them write their message of gratitude on the wings of their paper airplane.

3. Have students line up on one side of the room and fly their paper airplanes as far as they will go.

4. Each student then picks up an airplane that is not their own and reads the message. Take turns reading aloud or play music

and allow students time to read several different messages and soak in the joy.

DID YOU KNOW?

Promoting social comfort can reduce tensions between rival groups, cliques, and even rival gangs. Horacio Sanchez, author of *The Poverty Problem*, explains that helping students focus on things they have in common calms the amygdala's natural agitation toward anything that is unfamiliar or different from one's own experience.[41]

Stand if You Like... (All Ages)

This simple strategy helps build social comfort, which is especially important for groups that don't think they have anything in common. The rules are simple. Before beginning, introduce the response: "I knew I liked you for some reason." Then, the facilitator says, "Stand if you like..." followed by something commonly enjoyed (pizza, music, movies, sports, puppies, etc.). Everyone who is standing looks around and says, "I knew I liked you for some reason." Have everyone sit and repeat. If you need to, inject a little humor for those who haven't stood by saying, "Stand if you like sitting."

"I knew I liked you for some reason."

Pass the Message (All Ages)

Touch plays a critical role in turning on "connection mode" in the brain, so break out the hand sanitizer! This game can be great for resetting or reconnecting after a stressful time. You can circle up or just form lines close enough to reach the next person's hand. Similar to the game "telephone," one student will start a simple message of long or short hand squeezes. Students pass it along. Have fun seeing if the message stayed the same or changed. After this little bit of connection, teamwork, and laughter, this group is learning-ready! As an added bonus, this little game activates both sides of the body, waking up both sides of the brain.

PLAY FOR SOCIAL-EMOTIONAL LEARNING

Using this squirrel scale from @classcritters, how do you feel when you hear the letters S.E.L?[42] Whether you love social emotional learning, want to collapse like #5, or your Porcupine brain is kicking in like #6, I know you'll find something helpful in this section. If nothing else, try using this image as a check-in before class or staff meeting (color version is available to download). Beyond bringing some smiles and

On this squirrel scale, how do you feel today?

Class Critters   @1classcritter

SOURCE: @CLASSCRITTERS ON FACEBOOK

camaraderie, it can lead into a valuable SEL discussion. Have those who answered with the same number team up to discuss which part of their brain is on and what they need for their Upstairs Brains to be in charge for the next hour.

"My students are too old for this!" Play helps build connections in the brain by reducing barriers to learning and improving Upstairs Brain access. It doesn't have to be over-the-top silliness. Choose options from this section that fit your classroom or jot down your own ideas in the margins to add a little light-hearted SEL practice in your day.

Practice self-control with games, such as Jenga, freeze-tag, red light / green light, or Simon says. "Freeze Dance" is especially fun. The rules are simple: Dance while the music plays, and then FREEZE when the music stops.

Practice routines playfully. Have your students teach *you* about key parts of your classroom routines. Playfully do it wrong first and then ask for volunteers to help demonstrate the correct way. With younger students, try "forgetting" *wink* how to do things and let them help you do it right.

Use imagination to build empathy. Regardless of age, we activate the same pathways in the brain that are used in creative, make-believe play when we use our imaginations. "Let's imagine what it might be like for..." can be used in history, social studies, language arts, and beyond to build social emotional learning into academics.

Use imagination to support self-regulation and conflict resolution. Invite students to pretend they are directing themselves in a play. Whether dealing with test anxiety or working through a spat with a peer, practice taking a step back. What would the view of the situation be from the director's chair? What would you advise the actor playing you to do next? Maybe you even snag a second-hand director's chair to add in some movement. (Just don't treat it as a punitive timeout chair. That's a quick way to activate Downstairs Brain protectors!)

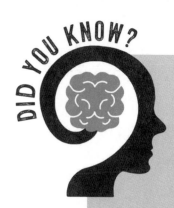

DID YOU KNOW?

Studies have shown that social make-believe play is an ideal context for cognitive development.[43] By creating imaginary situations, children:

- **Practice more advanced roles**
- **Practice using their thoughts to control their actions**
- **Pay attention to the feelings of others in a full body-brain manner**
- **Engage in creative problem-solving**

PLAY TO LEARN ANYTHING

Your students will remember more of what you are trying to teach if they are in a positive emotional state when they are learning.[44] Challenge is important too (more on that to come), but a little playfulness helps lessons "stick." Pepper some of these strategies into your week to help keep the Upstairs Brain engaged.

Use Stuffed Animals or Puppets (GR PreK-1)

A little owl on a stick helping kids practice their letter sounds is easier to pay attention to than *you* saying letter sounds for the umpteenth time. Pull this into story time, math facts, and beyond.

Get Moving with Games Like Hopscotch, Twister, and Hunt-and-Find (GR K-5)

These activities are perfect for practicing science vocab, math facts, language arts concepts, and more. Try hiding this week's sight words around the room. Have students bear walk around to find the next one, trace it with their finger, whisper it to themselves, and then bear walk to the next one. Adaptations might include having some students who have this set mastered crab walking around to be helpers.

PERIODIC TABLE TWISTER SOURCE: @KIDS_CHEM ON TWITTER

HOPSCOTCH SOURCE: @MAGICPI2 ON TWITTER

Play Digital Games (GR K-12)

Mix up your study time with a game on Kahoot, Blooket, Gimkit, or Quizizz. You may need to change the timing to make it fun for a variety of learning styles so that speed is not the only indicator of mastery.

Quiz and Find (GR 2-12)

Start a new topic by writing several categories of information or key concepts on the board. Have students write a question they don't know about one of those topics. Then instruct students to walk around to find someone who can answer the question, pausing to answer others' questions as well.

Rock-Paper-Scissors Study Time (GR 3-12)

Use this strategy when energy is lagging in the class or to study for a test. Students pair up, battle, and then the winner asks a quiz question or shares something they have learned so far in the lesson.

Include Creative Assignments Like Making a Board Game (GR 6-12)

Guess Who, Candy Land, and Chutes & Ladders are great options to let students showcase the concepts they have learned. It also cements their learning by getting more parts of the brain involved.

 *What can playfulness look like for you? What are you already doing that you want to keep doing? What other ideas do you want to try?*

POWERFUL PLAYFUL DE-ESCALATION STRATEGIES

Even with all the best brain-building keys in place, there will still be moments when students' Downstairs Brain protectors take over. When that happens, cognitive capacity narrows and reason goes offline.

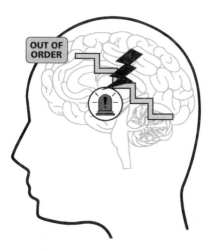

At this point, saying, "Use your coping skills" won't work. Try out these playful strategies to get the lights back on upstairs. Only then can we work to heal relationships, repair any damage done, and build Upstairs Brain coping skills.

"Isn't this rewarding bad behavior?" Remember, all behavior comes from the brain. If "bad behavior" is coming from a distressed brain, I want you to have all the tools available to soothe that little amygdala alarm and get the Upstairs Brain back in charge.

Humor

A little gesture of connection, a playful tone of voice, a good laugh...these are such powerful ways of waking up the Upstairs Brain when defense mode has taken over. Sometimes pulling the animal language in can help lessen the intensity of the situation:

- "Eek! Are those Porcupine spikes coming at me?"
- "Uh oh. I feel like Tiger brain is trying to take over. Can I help?"

Redirection / Distraction

The Downstairs Brain hyper focuses on what is wrong, and often its conclusion is...EVERYTHING IS WRONG! Instead of trying to use logic and reason that might lead to a power struggle, try this:

- **Change the subject.** This is especially effective when you bring up a topic you know the student enjoys. For example, mentioning anything related to plants and animals often helps my nature-loving son get through a Porcupine moment.

- **Give a task that helps them save face.** No one likes flipping their lid in front of peers. If you notice a student whose Tiger or Porcupine brain seems to be ramping up, grab any sheet of paper or stack of books lying around. In a tone of voice like you just remembered something, ask them to run it to the office or drop it off to the school counselor.

- **Ask about something not related to academics.**
  - Did you hear that thunderstorm last night?
  - Are you trying out for the school play again this year?

Remember, none of these options should be done in a punitive manner, or we will have lost the power of playfulness.

PLAYFUL TIPS AND SCRIPTS

Don't take yourself too seriously.

I don't mean you should be a pushover, but remember that even behavior that *feels* very personal usually isn't! Soften your face, relax your jaw, and take a breath.

Playfully use brain-based language.

- For younger students, that might sound like: "Uh-oh! I think your amygdala is saying, 'DANGER! DANGER!' And thinks I'm not on your team." If the student seems to be hearing you, try continuing with a little smile, "I'm sooo on your team, buddy. Do you think we can let your amygdala know?" If that kid gets back on track, remember to celebrate that Upstairs Brain skill of bouncing back from a tough moment.

- For older students, try something like: "Whoa! I am hearing amygdala alarms everywhere. It's like all our brain houses are on fire! What can we do to get things back on track?"

Deal with emotional contagion among staff.

We have all been in staff meetings or other situations when one bad mood seems to spread like a virus. Instead of ignoring the Porcupine moment or getting into a power struggle, try using a little playfulness to lighten the mood. Acknowledge that Porcupine brains might come out as we talk about the latest technology upgrade and call on the whole team to find some Upstairs Brain powers to help us through.

Play and playfulness are essential.

Find your style and roll with it! Pay attention to how others are receiving it in case you need to adjust a bit. For example, sarcasm can be fun, but it can also be hurtful. It's important to find the right balance.

And as my family has taught me, never underestimate the power of a well-timed fart joke.

KEY TAKEAWAYS

- Play has a profound impact on brain development.
- Play helps us build connection, nurturing the foundational building block of learning: Safe & Secure Relationships.
- Play doesn't have to be one more item on your to-do list. Instead, ideas in this chapter (and more that you glean from colleagues and your own experience) can enhance your teaching and reduce stress in the classroom.

- A little humor, redirection, or playful distraction can help de-escalate students who have spent a lot of time in The Mistrust Cycle.

DID YOU KNOW?

Laughter relieves tension, increases feel-good endorphins, and reduces stress.[45]

LOW-STRESS STARTING POINT

Start small if this is new territory for you.

Choose ONE idea from this chapter to try out this week. If you're feeling adventurous, try one from each section! Too much change at once will overwhelm you *and* your students. There's nothing wrong with starting small.

BE CURIOUS

Pay attention to your patterns. The way you learned to survive may not be the way you want to continue to live.

– Thelma Bryant-Davis, Ph.D.

Curiosity is innate. In a way, it's one of the first of our Upstairs Brain functions to develop. As we face stressors, though, it is easy for the Downstairs Brain to take over, prioritizing fierce power and control (Tiger brain) over curiosity. When problems seem too big, Turtle mode kicks in, shutting down curiosity *and* complex thought. But I promise you this: curiosity is in there—in you, in that student who never makes eye contact, and even in your grumpiest colleague.

GET TO KNOW YOUR TRIGGERS

Twenty years as a trauma therapist has taught me that the only way through the tough stuff is, well, through. We can't beat big feelings into submission. We can't run from life's challenges. We can't stuff down the pain forever. We must gently, safely, with connection and support, turn toward what IS. Luckily, we have some brain-based tools to support us on the journey.

In 1994, neuroscience researcher Dr. Stephen Porges introduced The Polyvagal Theory to better understand how the nervous system processes information.[46] His research found three hierarchical states related to the activation of the vagus or "wandering" nerve that connects many of the body's organs to the brain. Think of it as climbing up and down a ladder in our nervous system. In polyvagal terms, these three states are called Ventral Vagal, Sympathetic, and Dorsal Vagal. While the details of the theory and some of the terms might seem confusing at first, the principles deeply inform my understanding of the brain and body and can be quite helpful for understanding our behavior and emotions. Use this chart to add polyvagal language to your growing understanding of brain states and their related feelings and sensations.

	POLYVAGAL TERM	DESCRIPTION	COMMON FEELINGS	COMMON SENSATIONS
UPSTAIRS BRAIN	Ventral Vagal	Safe Steady Connected	Relaxed, thoughtful, open, creative, playful, curious, content, focused, joyful, grounded, ready, motivated, settled, interested, peaceful	Relaxed muscles, ease, lightness, energetic, free, mindfully aware
DOWNSTAIRS BRAIN	Sympathetic	Activated Fight-or-flight Distressed	Angry, worried, stressed, embarrassed, distracted, grumpy, upset, annoyed, panicky, nervous, frustrated	On edge, tense, hot, restless, guarded, under pressure, agitated, jumpy
DOWNSTAIRS BRAIN	Dorsal Vagal	Shutdown Immobilized Disconnected	Failure, shame, helpless, hopeless, overwhelmed, sad, vulnerable, lonely	Numb, stuck, heavy, cold, weak, slow, detached, foggy

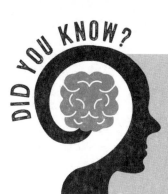

"Freeze" is a combined state of being both activated and shut down at the same time. Porcupine and Chameleon protectors tend to have this combined presentation. Play is also a combined state, with both activation and safe connection.[47] This is yet another reason play is such a power tool for strengthening the Upstairs Brain.

It is impossible to stay in that safe, steady, Upstairs Brain state every second. When little cues of danger (triggers) are picked up by the Downstairs Brain, the amygdala sends in your Downstairs Brain protectors. As I was talking this through with author and teacher Wendy Turner, she shared that identifying and naming her five biggest triggers and making plans for them was incredibly empowering in the classroom. "Something will go wrong and annoy me," she said. "If I don't go in knowing that, knowing my triggers and ready to be flexible, I'll end up in my Downstairs Brain. My power has nothing to do with the kids. My power is all about me having a plan and having skills to get through my five biggest triggers in the classroom."

"If I don't go in knowing that, knowing my triggers and ready to be flexible, I'll end up in my Downstairs Brain."

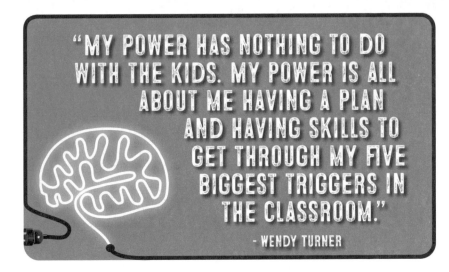

"MY POWER HAS NOTHING TO DO WITH THE KIDS. MY POWER IS ALL ABOUT ME HAVING A PLAN AND HAVING SKILLS TO GET THROUGH MY FIVE BIGGEST TRIGGERS IN THE CLASSROOM."

- WENDY TURNER

Since the word "triggers" means different things to different people, let's start with this working definition: triggers are cues of danger or threat in the environment detected by the Downstairs Brain with or without conscious thought. Common triggers include:

- Unmet basic needs (food, sleep, etc.)
- Sensory irritations
- Uncomfortable emotions like fear, embarrassment, or frustration
- A previous negative experience (whether we are conscious of it or not)
- Challenges to our values or beliefs
- Feeling like a failure
- Unmet expectations (whether realistic or not)

Dealing with triggers, traveling up and down the "stairs" in our nervous system, is a normal part of life. Sometimes, though, it seems like triggers are everywhere, especially in a room full of students (or staff)!

Think about your five biggest annoyances in your work or things that seem to overwhelm your resources. From tapping pens to missing homework to "talking back" to a new technology demand, everyone's triggers are different. What sends you into your Downstairs Brain?

My Triggers:

1. _____

2. _____

3. _____

4. _____

5. _____

What tools are in your toolbox to deal with these triggers? If you're not sure or it involves kicking a kid out of class, your homework is to ask a colleague or seek support to expand your plans and skills to get through these triggers.

_____

_____

_____

GLIMMERS AND ANCHORS

Thankfully, life isn't just about dealing with Downstairs Brain moments (our own or others'). Building on Dr. Porges' paradigm-shifting work, therapist Deb Dana introduced the concepts of "glimmers" and "anchors" to help people identify what "regulated" feels like.[48] Glimmers are small moments that spark joy, happiness, peace, or a sense that the world is ok, even for a fleeting moment. These are the people, pets, places, sensations, or observations that help the nervous system to feel safe or relaxed.[49] We can use these glimmers to rekindle joy or calm and find our way back to the solid ground of the Upstairs Brain. Anchors are the habits, memories, sensations, thoughts, or actions that help our nervous system experience safety and connection.[50] Training our brains to notice glimmers and find anchors helps steady us in the ups and downs of everyday life.

 *Think about what moments from today felt good or what makes you excited about your job. What makes you smile? Come back and add to the list as you notice more!*

My Glimmers:

_____

_____

_____

Is there a special person, place, or activity that helps you feel safe and secure? What gives you confidence? What starts your day off right or sets you up for a positive evening? What helps you feel steady?

My Anchors:

_____

_____

_____

BE CURIOUS ABOUT BIG FEELINGS

One of our most primal emotions—one that very quickly sends students into the Downstairs Brain operating mode—is fear, and it shows up in surprising ways.

Fear of...	Looks like...
Rejection or Abandonment	• Chameleon behavior, like following peer pressure or losing touch with their own interests or values • Not showing interest in connection ("I'll reject you before you can reject me.") • Trying too hard with peers and getting taken advantage of or getting in trouble • Constantly needing reassurance or physical proximity to an adult • Lashing out at adults, especially ones they are starting to feel close to • Hiding in screens (video games, social media, etc.)
Embarrassment or Confusion	• Running out the room • Angry outburst ("This is stupid.") • Personal attack ("I hate you.") • Joking or heckling • Refusing or avoiding work • Story telling or instinctual lying to protect from shame
Failure	• Not trying or giving up quickly • Complete Turtle shutdown (sleeping in class, not responding, etc.) • Anxiety or perfectionism • Stress and lack of enjoyment even in fun situations • Negative self-talk ("I suck at math.") • Low frustration tolerance or quick to anger even with small challenges
Negative Consequences or the Loss of Something Valued	• Saying what they wish were true • Hiding or running away from the situation • Zoning out or day dreaming • Shifting the attention or blame • Getting into a power struggle • An "I don't care" attitude
Unmet Needs or the Unknown	• Hyper-focused on material items • Stockpiling food or other resources • Difficulty sharing or thinking of others' feelings • Taking other people's belongings • Difficulty with change or transitions • Constant questioning and needing reassurance • Tiger moments about seemingly minor things

Use the following strategies to dig deeper into the big feelings behind big behaviors.

> Many students would benefit from doing these activities in alternative ways, such as verbally, through play, signs and symbols, typing, or a different preferred method of communication.

I Had a Moment (GR PreK-2)

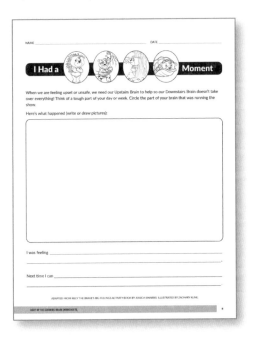

Become a Backpack Detective (GR 2-6)

1. Read *Hello, Anger* by Jessica Sinarski, illustrated by Macky Pamintuan.

2. Discuss the key themes highlighted in the book, such as:

    • Feeling angry is not bad—everyone feels mad sometimes!

- When we feel angry, there are usually other feelings underneath.

- Pausing to understand our body clues (sensations) and identify our feelings helps us deal with anger without hurting ourselves or others.

3. Have students discuss the characters' experiences. What situations from your own life feel similar to Ana, Ben, Grace, Katie, or Mrs. Miller? What happened when Mrs. Miller and her students didn't stop to check in with all the feelings underneath their anger?

4. Complete this activity individually or in groups.

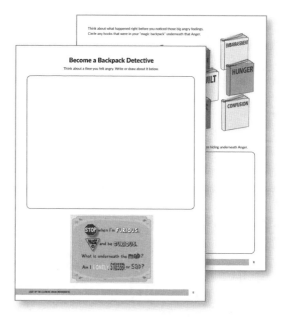

5. Repeat this rhyme often, especially when *you* are starting to feel furious!

Stop when I'm furious. Pause and be curious.
What is underneath the mad? Am I lonely, stressed, or sad?

Glimmers and Triggers (GR 6-12)

Help your secondary students build some self-awareness with their own glimmer and trigger activity. Have students apply what they discover via group discussion, conferences, or even in a writing assignment.

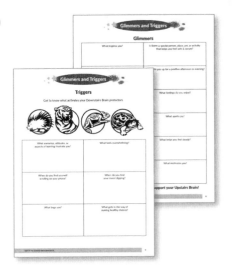

WHAT IS THE NEED?

We have all seen big feelings and big behaviors disrupt learning. While it is normal for your Downstairs Brain to want to control and/or punish those disruptive behaviors, let's keep bringing a brain-based lens to this issue. Will harsh punishments help build a student's Upstairs Brain capacity? Nope. Will shame and blame help? Definitely not. Is it a character issue? Not really.

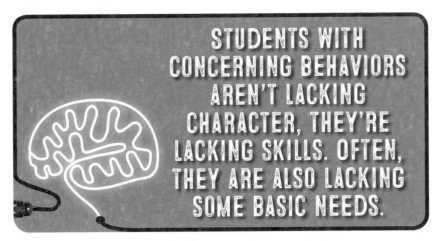

STUDENTS WITH CONCERNING BEHAVIORS AREN'T LACKING CHARACTER, THEY'RE LACKING SKILLS. OFTEN, THEY ARE ALSO LACKING SOME BASIC NEEDS.

Research shows that detention, suspension, restraints, and seclusion are outdated behavior management strategies that neither build skills nor meet needs.[51] These punitive measures leave everyone stuck in survival brain, leading to more big feelings and dysregulated behavior.

Dr. Ross Greene, internationally-known author, researcher, and educational consultant, has worked with kids with explosive behaviors for over thirty years. Instead of focusing on the problematic behavior, he encourages schools and families to notice lagging skills and unmet needs.[52] The idea of behavior being tied to human needs is nothing new, though our understanding of what those needs really are continues to grow and change. Use this guide to start thinking more deeply about the need behind the behavior.

1. **Basic need check—are they tired or hungry?** There have been times I was about to lock horns with my one of my dynamic, strong-willed kiddos only to realize that he was hangry and not thinking straight (or I was). So, I paused the battle, handed him a snack, and, with compassion, named the feeling: "Bud, you're so hungry that it's hard to think. Same thing happens to me. It's so frustrating." Taking this into school might look like:

   - Making sure kids have had breakfast before they start class

   - Having a supply of healthy snacks that are available before defense brain kicks in

   - Reaching out to parents if a young student seems tired

   - Brainstorming with older students about how they can get more sleep at night

2. **Felt safety check—what messages am I sending with my face, tone of voice, and posture?**

- Relax your forehead and unclench your jaw. Sometimes if I want to yell, I will sing what I want to say so I keep myself more regulated. It doesn't have to be a fancy song:

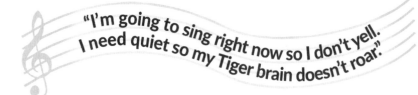

"I'm going to sing right now so I don't yell. I need quiet so my Tiger brain doesn't roar."

- Hold out "roaaaaar" like an opera singer, and I promise you'll have the class's attention without sending anyone into defense mode!

- "Low and slow" or a side-by-side posture can be helpful when a kiddo is dysregulated.

- Be curious. Are there other things in the environment that might be sending threat messages?

3. **Is there a co-regulation need?** Could a moment of connection with you, peers, or another trusted adult help get the Upstairs Brain back online? A little playfulness or an opportunity for some emotional release might be just what's needed!

4. **Sensory need check—are they stuck or agitated or bouncing off the walls?** Use all your great tools from Key Two to check in with the senses.

5. **Do they understand what you are expecting in the moment?** You would be amazed how many times "misbehavior" is rooted in miscommunication! Slow down and be clear. Practice routines, playfully go through the steps of tasks, and regularly review expectations in an encouraging way.

6. **Do they need to feel seen and heard?** I'm reminded of the video by Clint Pulver, who shared that he struggled to hold

still in school.[53] As a young boy, his incessant tapping was getting on everyone's nerves and landing him in the principal's office. He tried

SOURCE: HTTPS://YOUTU.BE/4P5286T_KN0

to hold still, tried to sit on his hands, but it wasn't working. When Mr. Jensen told him to stay after class, he thought he was in trouble again. Instead of criticizing Clint, Mr. Jensen got curious: "Have you ever thought about playing the drums?" Pulling a pair of drumsticks out of his desk as the music in the video swells, Mr. Jensen says, "Hey, Clint. You're not a problem. I think you're a drummer." Mr. Jensen was right. Clint went on to get a full-ride scholarship as a drummer and built a successful career, thanks in no small part to that pivotal moment with Mr. Jensen. He truly *saw* Clint instead of just seeing the annoying behavior.

7. **Does this student (or staff member) need another chance, a different option, or some skill-building to be successful?** If yes, offer it, and watch that Upstairs Brain grow!

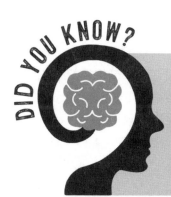

DID YOU KNOW?

Talking (or communicating in some fashion) and movement are needs.[54] As much as you may want kids to just sit still and be quiet, that really shouldn't be the goal!

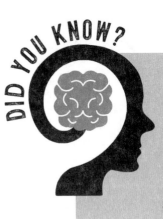

BUT WHAT ABOUT CONSEQUENCES?!

For far too long in the world of education—and in general in this country—we have relied on punishments and consequences to "manage behavior." But when a brain is in survival mode, a sticker chart isn't going to cut it. Yelling and scolding won't help. Taking away recess won't get the Upstairs Brain back in charge. Detention and suspension definitely won't do it.

Where does that leave us? There are underlying questions here that our growing brain-based skills will help us untangle. The thought, "But what about consequences?" can come from different parts of the brain. Your Upstairs Brain may genuinely be asking, "How do I help hold this child accountable for their actions?" or "What would help this student reflect, learn, and grow so that they can be successful?" Usually, however, the adult's Tiger or Porcupine brain protectors are feeling unsafe, worried, offended, hurt, and MAD, which is understandable. The brain's natural response when the amygdala detects a threat is to jump to defense mode. *Tiger powers, activate! How can I roar and puff so this student doesn't do this again?* Okay, that's probably not exactly what you're thinking, but there are thoughts coming from that same protective place, such as:

> "Shut it down. This is hurting the other kids. I need to protect them from this threat."

> "They know better and did it anyway. It's their parents' fault. No discipline at home so I need to teach them a lesson here."

Failure is another common feeling lurking below the surface when we are faced with big behaviors in students. Instead of being curious about how we can collaborate, learn, and better support the child, our Downstairs Brain protectors are ready to rush in and defend with thoughts like:

> *Failure is another common feeling lurking below the surface when we are faced with big behaviors in students.*

> "I don't have enough letters after my name to deal with this. Get this kid out of my class."

> "That kid is messed up. I'll just survive the year and then they'll be someone else's problem."

> "I don't get paid enough to deal with this *bleep*—I'm out."

The Downstairs Brain favors power and control over cooperation and collaborative problem-solving. No wonder our thoughts are quick to jump to punishment and harsh consequences! Discipline, on the other hand, means "to teach." Let's compare the two:

Discipline	Punishment
Instilled in children by trusted adults	Imposed on children
Preventive	Punitive
Proactive	Reactive
Child learns self-control and accountability	Adult is responsible to try to control the child's behavior
Offers structure and guidance	Imposes demands that don't necessarily repair any damage done
Encourages desired behavior	Focuses on undesired behavior
Teaches the preferred way to solve or prevent problems	Does not teach preferred or expected behaviors
Encourages children to be capable and responsible for making decisions	Imposes decisions on children
Protects and nurtures children	May cause emotional and physical pain
Fosters self-esteem and confidence	Reinforces poor self-esteem (especially if the punishment is demeaning)
Children rely on their own inner controls or rules for conduct (growing self-regulation)	Responsible behavior is expected only when authority figures are present
Children and adults have cooperative, shared, positive relationships	Children learn to avoid and fear adults

WHAT WOULD HELP THIS STUDENT REFLECT, LEARN, AND GROW SO THAT THEY CAN REPAIR (IF NECESSARY) AND BE MORE SUCCESSFUL GOING FORWARD?

Create more brain-aligned discipline and accountability in your classroom, school, and district by using this guiding question: What would help this student reflect, learn, and grow so that they can repair (if necessary) and be more successful going forward? For example, if a student is struggling with turning in homework on time, be curious! What is making it difficult to get assignments in on time?

- Does the student need help developing planning and organization skills? Work with the supports in your school to help this student learn and practice these important executive function skills.

- Are there factors at home that are making evenings difficult? Perhaps they would benefit from having some time and space during or after school to get work done.

- Are they struggling with the mechanics of getting the papers or files in the right place? If so, try practicing playfully, working with a buddy, or relearning the procedures and then teaching one of their safe adults.

All of these strategies are going to be more effective than scolding, taking away recess, or docking points off their grade. And there's the added benefit that you are helping them build critical connections in their brain that will help them not only be better homework-turner-inners, but also develop the executive function skills they will need for adult life.

BRING CURIOSITY HOME

Each school has a unique student body and community of parents, guardians, and other invested adults. Use these strategies to broaden your curiosity about your students' families and trusted adults. These practices reinforce the cornerstone of all learning: safe and secure relationships.

Safe, Seen, and Valued

This simple communication helps parents and caregivers know that their experience matters, which is critical if you want to nurture a collaborative relationship. Send this by email, create a quick survey, or send home the following form found in your digital downloads.

Hello!

I'm excited to have your child in my class. I know that my students learn best when they sense that they are safe, seen, and valued and I will do my best to create a classroom community that fosters these needs. I also want you to know how much your experience and expertise about your student matters to me! Please fill out and return this form to help me create a culture of belonging this year.

_____
STUDENT'S NAME

_____
YOUR NAME

_____
RELATIONSHIP TO STUDENT

What have you / your student loved about school in the past?
_____
_____
_____

What has bothered you / your student about school?
_____
_____
_____

Thank you for sharing your time and energy with me. Looking forward to a great year ahead!

Sincerely,

Tell Me Something GREAT About Your Kid

Include this activity in your back-to-school night by grabbing sticky notes, something for parents to write with, and a big piece of paper. At the top, add your prompt, such as "Tell me something GREAT about your kid." Write clear instructions nearby so parents know what to do:

- Take a sticky note
- Write your child's name
- Write down something wonderful!

Just like that, you have some great data to start your year with this group of kids. If possible, reach out to parents and caregivers who were not able to attend with the same question.

SOURCE: K. HOLLEY, ED.S, @KHOLLEYEDS ON TWITTER, ORIGINAL SOURCE UNKNOWN[55]

Five Photos

While collaboration between parents and educators is critical for student success, there are often big feelings involved. IEP meetings, conferences, and other interactions are often focused on deficits, challenging behaviors, and other sensitive topics. Neurodiversity expert Thomas Armstrong encourages the use of photos as a starting point for discussion in a meeting. With photos typically stored on phones, this is easier than ever. Simply ask parents/caregivers to bring or send in five photos of their child. Armstrong notes, "Parents will usually bring in photos of their child doing positive things, which can indicate particular abilities or strengths." Begin your meeting connecting with the child and family through these photos to nurture that "Safe and Secure Relationships" building block even in a stressful setting like an IEP meeting.

SIMPLE SCRIPTS TO SPARK CURIOSITY

I wonder...

The call to be curious sometimes leads people to interrogation mode: "Why did you do that? What were you thinking? And then what happened?" This is a quick way to foster animosity and disconnection rather than promoting Upstairs Brain functioning. Curiosity coming from the Upstairs Brain will sound lighter.[56] Even with difficult topics, the tone is that there's a mystery to solve, and we are in it together!

- "Huh? I wonder what was going on there?"

- "Uh-oh. Looks like your legs want to run out of the room when we start math. It's so hard. I'm curious what helps you when you're working with these confusing numbers."

- "Hey, *insert student's name*. Seems like you're having a tough time staying awake in class. Let's brainstorm." Follow-up questions as you explore might include things like:

  – "How's your sleep at night?"

- "Does it happen more when we get to certain parts of the lesson?"
- "When do you find yourself the most awake and interested in what we're doing?"

What's good?

Our brains naturally focus on the negative. Just like we want to work from a strength-based mindset with students, let's train our brains to notice the good in everyday life.

- Start a text or email chain with a few colleagues where you share positive moments from your day. This doesn't mean you can't connect and get support with the tough stuff. It just actively makes space for the good!

- Using a journal or a notes app on your phone, start a list of good things in your life and add to it every day. Repeat entries welcome! Mine includes, in no particular order, warm shower, new panda PJs, snuggles with my boys, the tree outside my window, essential oils, Diet Coke on ice, my pillow...you get the idea!

- Take a "What's good?" break in class or start staff meetings by making space for everyone to share something positive. Set a group goal of ten responses before you move on to the next topic. Be sure to provide options to include those who prefer to write or share their thoughts in non-verbal ways.

Practice the pause

In a heated moment, it's usually the things we say that we regret. Take a little advice from *Fostering Resilient Learners* author Kristin Souers: **"When in doubt, shut your mouth and take a breath."**[57]

A regular mindfulness or meditation practice is a great way to increase your curiosity capacity and reduce the impact of stress. Practicing the pause in everyday moments establishes a pathway in the brain that will make it easier to feel steady and in control during a crisis.

KEY TAKEAWAYS

- Getting to know your triggers is a critical part of becoming the boss of your brain.

- Paying attention to glimmers and anchors strengthens the Upstairs Brain.

  - Glimmers are small moments that spark joy, happiness, peace, or a sense that the world is okay. This helps the nervous system to feel safe and calm.

  - Anchors are the habits, memories, sensations, thoughts, and actions that help steady you.

- Fear can show up in surprising ways. Understanding our relationship to this primal feeling will help us think before we act. Use the tools in this chapter to help your staff and students do the same.

- Students with concerning behaviors don't lack character; they lack skills. Often, they also lack some basic needs.

- Create more brain-aligned discipline and accountability in your classroom, school, and district by using this guiding question: *"What would help this student reflect, learn, and grow so that they can repair (if necessary) and be more successful going forward?"*

- Instead of going into interrogation mode, remember that you and your student(s) are on the same team. Even with difficult topics, use the tone that there's a mystery to solve and you are going to figure it out together!

LOW-STRESS STARTING POINT

Get to know your glimmers and triggers.

If you haven't already, go back and complete one or both of the reflection exercises at the beginning of this chapter. The rest of the book will wait.

CREATE A CULTURE OF SAFETY

I received an email from my son's superintendent with a quote that resonated with me so much that I immediately bought the book, *Belonging through a Culture of Dignity: The Keys to Successful Equity Implementation*. "Belonging isn't just a nice sentiment or a word on a Hallmark greeting card," write authors Floyd Cobb and John Krownapple. "It's a need that's hardwired into human beings. Like neglecting the need for food or water, neglecting belonging is hazardous to our health. In fact, it's lethal."[58]

In a way, creating a culture of safety is the first key. But many of the practices that cultivate safety and belonging are built on an understanding of the brain and our eight senses. It requires the

> *In a way, creating a culture of safety is the first key.*

comfort and joy of playfulness and the open-minded acceptance of curiosity. If you skipped ahead to this chapter, I get it! We all long to feel safe, seen, and valued. But I encourage you to go back. Spend some time understanding and implementing the foundational elements from the previous chapters so that you can make the most of the safety-building strategies found in the pages ahead.

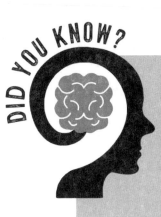

Felt safety is a subjective sense of safety.[59] You experience felt safety on a subconscious level based on the information coming into your brain from outside your body, inside your body, and between you and the people around you.

FELT SAFETY: THE BRAIN SPEAKS NON-VERBAL

Your nervous system is constantly asking one big question to determine which part of the brain will be in charge: Am I safe? Or, more accurately,

is there *any* sign of danger or threat? Do I feel safe enough for the slower "Think Before Acting" part of my brain to run things? Dr. Steven Porges coined the term "neuroception" to define this subconscious scanning for signals of safety and danger that our nervous systems are doing *multiple times per second*.[60] While your nervous system is looking for any actual threats to your life, more often it picks up on perceived or potential danger, such as:

- Rejection
- Embarrassment
- Confusion
- Failure

- Loss of something valued
- The unknown
- Abandonment
- Negative consequences
- Something that doesn't line up with our identity or perception of self

The Downstairs Brain does not see a difference between perceived threats and actual dangers, which leads to a lot of "false alarms." For kids who have spent time in The Mistrust Cycle, those false alarms can lead to some problematic behaviors. Whether the amygdala's split-second assessment is accurate or not, the result is that, without a lot of intentional brain building, the "Act Without Thinking" part of the brain runs our lives. We see this in our polarized politics, fragmented family relationships, and struggling schools.

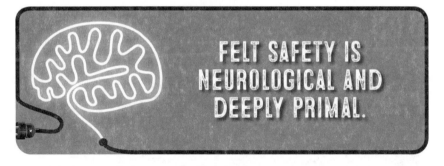

FELT SAFETY IS NEUROLOGICAL AND DEEPLY PRIMAL.

Felt safety is neurological and deeply primal. It is easy for moments of disconnection to become a way of life. Fortunately, there are simple strategies that can help students experience felt safety in your classroom, school hallways, and even in situations when brain-aligned discipline is necessary. In addition to getting the senses involved using the tools provided in previous chapters, nurture felt safety in the following ways:

- Ensure access to food and water.

- Muster some warmth in your eyes.

- Avoid yelling or scolding. Try using a playful or matter-of-fact tone of voice. The varied, melodic cadence called "mother-ese" can also be helpful. During a Tiger moment, try matching your student's intensity *without the anger*. With compassion and a little energy, say, "UGH! I get it!! Let's walk it off."

- Keep your body language open and non-threatening. Head-to-head tends to feel confrontational while side-by-side sends messages of support.

- Be predictable. Good surprises might be fun now and then, but in general, brains like to know what to expect.

- Movement, rhythm, and music are helpful for cultivating felt safety.

- Use the respectful, brain-based language found in this book.

One striking example of the power of this shame-reducing language took place in a women's prison I visited in 2018. I was invited there to lead a workshop for a group of incarcerated moms. We used the book *Riley the Brave* to open some discussion about parenting, trauma, and the brain. We talked about Porcupine and Turtle moments and all the primal feelings that seem to take over out of the blue. It made sense to this group, many of whom were sitting around that table because of some pretty big Tiger moments.

We were finishing up when one of the women next to me, Janet, suddenly stood up. Linda, sitting next to her, barked, "SIT DOWN!" Linda and I shared a sideways glance, and she said, "Wait was that... Porcupine? Or Tiger?"

"I think so," I said with a hint of a smile. "What do you think might have sparked that?"

Janet was still standing and anxiously tapping her foot. Linda turned to her and said, a little awkwardly, "I'm afraid you're going to get in trouble for standing up."

Janet responded in a matter-of-fact tone, "I don't believe you," and sat back down. What could have been a tense, combative moment based in fear was diffused with this deceptively simple framework. I heard from the social worker afterward that she continued to hear inmates mentioning Porcupine and Tiger moments long after my visit. Even in a setting as stressful, toxic, and fear-inducing as prison, this language is freeing.

SAFETY FOR STRESSED BRAINS

Colby's mother sat in my office in tears. "We spent 20 minutes at the 'sneak peek' night, and Colby's teacher didn't make eye contact with the kids once." Colby had been struggling in PreK, and his mom was worried about how kindergarten would go. He didn't have his letters down like his big sister did at this age. One of his preschool teachers had described him as "defiant" and complained to his mom about how he wouldn't sit still during lessons. Colby's dad had ADHD and Dyslexia, and his parents thought Colby might too. When I started seeing the family, it seemed there were also some sensory processing challenges making it difficult for Colby to feel safe and regulated.

On day three of kindergarten, the first phone call came. "The principal called me," his mom said. "Apparently, he took a toy back to his desk during reading. His teacher said he was stealing and sent him to the principal." The tone continued to be punitive, and the expectations were unrealistic for any young child, but especially a kiddo like Colby. He got out of line in the hallway and was sent to the principal's office again. Four times in the first seven days of school, Colby was sent out of his classroom. An emotionally crushed little guy entered my office that Thursday afternoon. We played together as he stuck near mom. I learned that his latest scolding at school included some yelling and heaps more shame. It was clear that things were not going well in room 114, and a change was needed.

Colby's parents jumped into action and were able to get him into a different class. "On the very first day," his mom reported, "he came out with a smile on his face." The next time I saw him, Colby proudly showed me a big piece of paper with "COLBY" spelled out in dot paint.

"Wow!" I remarked with a smile. "It spells your name. That's so cool."

"Yeah," he said proudly. "I'm a *very* special boy."

Colby's experience with his new teacher, Miss G, demonstrated the power of putting brain science in action. She prioritized safe and secure relationships above all. When Colby had a Downstairs Brain moment, she got on his level, calmly reminded him that he was safe, and "we keep each other safe here." Within a couple of days, the behavior reported in his first classroom had disappeared.

COLBY WAS A *STRESSED* KID, NOT A *BAD* KID.

Miss G recognized that Colby was a *stressed* kid, not a *bad* kid. She got him into a reading group that worked at his skill level, with lots of play and multi-sensory components built in. She worked with the whole class on building stress management and self-regulation skills. They practiced "going with the group plan" and talking about their feelings. Miss G shared the language with Colby's parents so they could reinforce the principles at home. The tone was supportive and kind instead of punitive and harsh. Miss G provided the safety that Colby's stressed brain needed.

BUILDING TRUST WITH NEURODIVERGENT STUDENTS

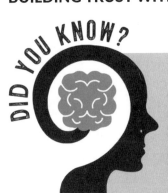

DID YOU KNOW?

"Autism is not an illness. It's a different way of being human," according to Dr. Barry Prizant and many autistic adults who have pushed for a celebration of their differences instead of a focus on what's "wrong," or missing. That's why many people discourage the use of the puzzle piece imagery related to autism. Not only is it tied to some problematic awareness campaigns that presented autism as a tragic disease much like cancer, but it also represents the view of autistic people as "puzzling." Altogether Autism's former autistic advisor Paula Jessop explains, "We don't wish to be viewed as akin to a puzzle that can't be worked out."[61]

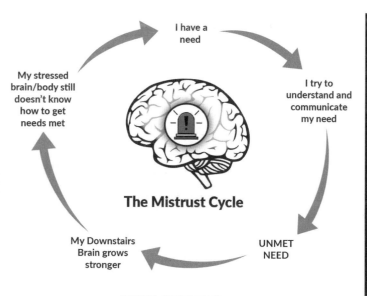

Unfortunately, Colby's experience is all-too common for neurodivergent students. Trying to survive in a world that feels confusing and overstimulating leads to high stress and dysregulation. So often, the goal becomes controlling behavior instead of helping the student feel safe, seen, and valued. Dr. Barry Prizant is among the world's leading authorities on autism and neurodevelopmental conditions with more than fifty years of experience as a clinician, researcher, educator, and consultant. He notes that autistic people face tremendous obstacles to building trust. Remember, our brains are constantly scanning for danger outside our bodies, inside via our hidden senses, and between us and other people. I have yet to meet a neurodivergent person who hasn't spent a little time in The Mistrust Cycle.

DISTRESS, DYSREGULATION & DISCONNECTION

DISTRESS & DYSREGULATION

I have a need

I try to understand and communicate my need

My stressed brain/body still doesn't know how to get needs met

The Mistrust Cycle

UNMET NEED

My Downstairs Brain grows stronger

SOURCE: JESSICA SINARSKI

We can interrupt this cycle! In his book, *Uniquely Human*, Dr. Prizant recommends the following five strategies to help autistic and other neurodivergent individuals foster trusting relationships.[62]

1. Acknowledge attempts to communicate.

2. Practice shared control to build self-determination.

3. Acknowledge the individual's emotional state.

4. Be dependable, reliable, and clear.

5. Celebrate successes.

Think of a neurodivergent student or staff member you have seen flip into protection mode. What would it look like to put one of Dr. Prizant's trust-building strategies into practice with that person?

EQUITY, DIVERSITY, AND A CULTURE OF BELONGING

Do the best you can until you know better.
Then when you know better, do better.

– Maya Angelou

I'm guessing some readers want to skip over this section and some are wondering why I haven't been talking about this *more*. Let me start by repeating Albus Dumbledore's wise words: "Fear of a name increases fear of the thing itself."[63] So, let's begin this section by naming a few things so they don't have to be unknown and scary.

CULTURE	the norms, values, beliefs, traditions, and rituals of a group built up over time	"Culture is the way we do things around here." - Cobb & Krownapple[64]
EQUITY	fairness, justice	It is not about everyone getting the same thing (equality) but recognizing that we must make adjustments where we find injustice or unfair disadvantages.[65]
DIVERSITY	the state of being diverse; variety	"Diversity is not a vision to move toward but a reality to recognize and acknowledge." - Cobb & Krownapple[66]
IMPLICIT BIAS	a form of bias (attitudes, behaviors, and actions that are prejudiced in favor of or against one person or group compared to another) that occurs automatically and unintentionally, that nevertheless affects judgments, decisions, and behaviors[67]	Because of the lack of awareness inherent in implicit bias, this can be difficult to detect. In fact, you may consciously express that you feel the opposite (using your Upstairs Brain) while you act without thinking (Downstairs Brain) in ways that negatively impact others.
PRIVILEGE	a special right, advantage, or immunity granted or available only to a particular person or group[68]	Just like many of these terms, the word 'privilege' often sparks a strong reaction such as, "Privilege? Do you know how hard my life has been?!" Benefitting from White Privilege does not mean that life has been easy. It makes sense that you want your struggle and ability to overcome to be acknowledged or honored. After all, we all need to feel safe, seen, and valued to function at our best. I encourage a broadening of this thought... you have worked hard and accomplished a lot, AND, if you are White in this country, you have benefitted from laws and practices designed for and by White people. Hard work and privilege. Both can be true.
RACISM	a belief that race is a fundamental determinant of human traits and capacities and that racial differences produce an inherent superiority of a particular race[69]	Because of implicit bias, however, this definition seems more helpful: "A powerful collection of policies that sustains racial inequities or injustices and is substantiated by ideas of racial hierarchy." - Kendi & Stone[70]
RACIST (ADJ)	of, relating to, or characterized by racism[71]	In *How to Be a (Young) Antiracist*, authors Kendi and Stone point out that while "racist" is often used as a noun (i.e. "He's a racist."), it may be more constructive as an adjective. This will enable us to notice and name the racist ideas, policies, or practices that impede equity work.[72]

As a White, heterosexual, cisgender woman, I am part of the majority demographic for teachers.[73] While this section is for everyone, I am especially hopeful that readers who are still on the journey of recognizing the privileges we have benefited from and unlearning implicit bias will find renewed energy to foster a culture of belonging for each member of our diverse school communities.

I was sitting on a patch of short grey carpet, tucked in some corner of a college campus building with five other first-year students, when I first read Peggy McIntosh's 1989 article, "White Privilege: Unpacking the Invisible Knapsack." Among other thoughtful reflections about her unearned privilege, McIntosh listed 26 areas where she personally enjoyed some comfort and ease compared to her Black colleagues, such as:

- When I am told about our national heritage or about "civilization," I am shown that people of my color made it what it is.

- I can arrange to protect my children most of the time from people who might not like them.

- I can speak in public to a powerful male group without putting my race on trial.

- I can choose blemish cover or bandages in "flesh" color and have them more or less match my skin.[74]

McIntosh went on to write, "I was taught to see racism only in individual acts of meanness, not in invisible systems conferring dominance on my group." If your brain just went into defense mode, notice the sensations and thoughts. Words like "racism" and "dominance" can set off your amygdala alarm, but we need our curious, connection-seeking Upstairs Brains for this conversation. Nearly 35 years after this article was written, the debate still rages, with many White people's amygdala's screaming, "But I'm not racist!" The fact remains, however, that students of color, students with disabilities, and students who identify as LGBTQ+ are most at risk for suspensions and expulsions, a key part of the "school-to-prison-pipeline" that no educator wants to perpetuate.[75]

While it may be true that most professionals do not *intentionally* discriminate, when it comes to the disproportionate suspension rates of Black and Latino students, research has shown that school leaders' beliefs and teachers' implicit biases play a stronger role than actual student behavior.[76,77,78] With what we know about the brain, this makes sense. Brains love putting things into categories and making processes automatic. There's no time to sort through all 11 million bits of data coming in every second, so we get very good at acting without thinking. This is part of why creating equity, embracing diversity, and establishing a culture of safety are so difficult. It is easy to get stuck in the "Dysfunctional Cycle of Equity Work."

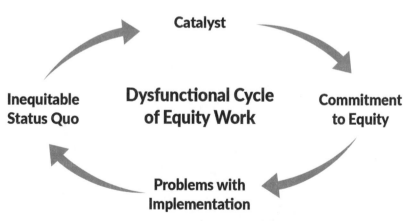

SOURCE: DR. FLOYD COBB AND JOHN KROWNAPPLE IN
BELONGING THROUGH A CULTURE OF DIGNITY[79]

The Dysfunctional Cycle of Equity Work

Does this sound familiar? There's an "incident" or crunching of the numbers that points to a problem. That leads to statements of belief, committees, and consultants. After a few sweeping trainings, there is frustration about the lack of progress, the slow pace of change, or the esoteric nature of training on these emotion-laden topics. That leads right back to business as usual, the inequitable status quo. And round and round we go. It doesn't have to be like this.

This brings me to one more important definition: "We define **belonging** as **the extent to which people feel appreciated, validated, accepted, and treated fairly within an environment (e.g. school, classroom, or work)**," write Cobb and Krownapple. "When students feel that they belong, they aren't worried and distracted about being treated as a stereotype or a thin slice of their multidimensional identities."[80]

Yes! Belonging is being appreciated, valued, accepted, and treated fairly. Brains are alert to differences. We can let that send us into defense mode or use it for good. Therefore, the work is big *and* small, systemic *and* personal. No community member silenced, minimized, or marginalized, but rather a rich culture of belonging, where it is safe to be me and safe to be you. This is at the heart of equity, diversity, and creating a culture of safety.

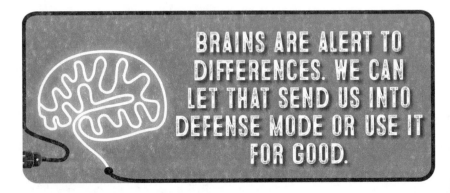

BRAINS ARE ALERT TO DIFFERENCES. WE CAN LET THAT SEND US INTO DEFENSE MODE OR USE IT FOR GOOD.

SAFETY IN DIFFICULT MOMENTS

Keep it simple in moments of intense stress.

The Downstairs Brain has limited capacity for language and complex thought. Choose a short phrase or two that you can use when Downstairs Brains are taking over, such as:

- I'm going to take a breath.
- I think we're both having a hard time.
- Let's cool off.
- Let's back up. (If you have enough Upstairs Brain power to be playful, try saying "Reverse, Reverse" in your best "Cha-cha slide" voice).
- I need to reset.

Shoulders—Breath—Face

Practice this miniature upper body scan often. With repeated use, it will become a reliable 10-second reset strategy.

 Roll your shoulders forward, up, and around, letting them settle down your back.

 As you do that, breathe in deeply, pause, and slowly expel all the air from your lungs.

 At the end of your long exhale, let your face relax. Release any tension in your forehead and temples, allowing a slight smile to form.

After you get the hang of it, teach and practice with your whole class or group.

Stop, Drop, and Roll

Whether you are feeling the sting of someone else's Downstairs Brain moment or afraid you might flip your lid, this strategy from trauma expert Resmaa Menakem will help protect you from the flames.[81]

STOP: Whatever you are doing, thinking, or saying, stop! Don't go any further down the same emotional and mental path.

DROP BACK: Pay attention to what you feel, what's going on around you, and where you seem to be headed. Be curious. Is that where you want to go? If not, say so out loud: "Let's not go where I think we're headed. Let's figure out something different."

ROLL: Whatever happens next in your body, let it happen. You might cry or laugh or moan or sigh. Unless it will harm you or someone else, let the feeling roll on through. You don't have to fight it, run from it, or cut it off.

Notice that this practice doesn't make the uncomfortable problem go away, but it DOES keep us from lighting more fires on top. Practice it with staff and teach your students.

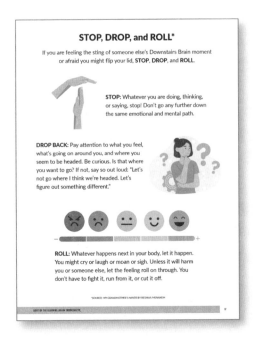

STOP, DROP, and ROLL*

If you are feeling the sting of someone else's Downstairs Brain moment or afraid you might flip your lid, **STOP, DROP,** and **ROLL.**

STOP: Whatever you are doing, thinking, or saying, stop! Don't go any further down the same emotional and mental path.

DROP BACK: Pay attention to what you feel, what's going on around you, and where you seem to be headed. Be curious. Is that where you want to go? If not, say so out loud: "Let's not go where I think we're headed. Let's figure out something different."

ROLL: Whatever happens next in your body, let it happen. You might cry or laugh or moan or sigh. Unless it will harm you or someone else, let the feeling roll on through. You don't have to fight it, run from it, or cut it off.

SOURCE: MY GRANDMOTHER'S HANDS BY RESMAA MENAKEM

When the door closes, find the window.

When you feel like your only options are punitive or, despite your best efforts, the material is not sinking in, it can feel like all the doors are closing. Trauma-Invested Institute founders Kristin Souers and Pete Hall encourage educators to find the window.[82]

- Take a deep breath and check in with your fears and concerns.
- Ask three trusted colleagues for their suggestions.
- Search online or in your professional learning spaces.
- Team up with an administrator to think through possible solutions.
- Sometimes a good night of sleep and a healthy meal will clear the cobwebs, and suddenly that window appears!

Remember—the brain speaks nonverbal.

Check in with what you are communicating with your face (especially eyes!), your tone of voice, and your posture or body language. Also, check in with what your curriculum, books in the library, and choice of guest speakers are saying nonverbally. Representation matters!

KEY TAKEAWAYS

- Felt safety is the deeply personal, primal, and automatic response to your brain's repeated question: Am I safe? Your nervous system is constantly scanning for signs of danger or perceived threat, such as rejection, confusion, and negative consequences.
- Talking about Downstairs Brain moments in animal terms can reduce shame and blame.

- Actions coming from a stressed brain might look like "bad behavior." When you notice this, focus on bolstering the foundational building blocks of learning: Safe & Secure Relationships, Stress Management, and Self-Regulation.

- Most neurodivergent students have spent time in The Mistrust Cycle and benefit from intentional trust-building practices in the school setting.

- Brains are alert to differences. We can let that send us into defense mode or allow our increased awareness to compel us toward fostering equity, honoring diversity, and creating a culture of belonging for all members of the school community.

- There are many strategies for finding safety in difficult moments and responding in ways that will de-escalate the situation. At a minimum, try to check in with what your face (especially your eyes), your tone of voice, and your posture/ body language are communicating.

LOW-STRESS STARTING POINT

Offer more opportunities for felt safety.

Look over the ideas listed for nurturing felt safety in the school setting. What are you already doing that you want to continue? What is an area you want to grow? One trick for learning new skills is to find someone who is good at a particular skill and observe them. Get curious. Ask for their help as you work on building that new skill.

SHARE THE POWER

> *A child's mind is not a container to be filled*
> *but rather a fire to be kindled.*

– Dorothea Brande

If you are thinking, "Share the power? Students need to follow teachers' directions. Period." I hear you. And I get it. There are certainly times that I want my kids to just, for the love of all that is good in the universe, do what I say! Hearing "no" or being ignored does not feel good! Adults often feel dismissed, hurt, humiliated, angry, threatened, or even powerless, which understandably sets off our Downstairs Brain

> *Hearing "no" or being ignored does not feel good!*

protectors. The more we apply a brain-based lens, however, the more we realize there are times when kids *can't* follow directions. At least not in that moment or not exactly in the way we want them to. Incidents of defiance usually have more to do with what is going on in that student's little brain than any interest in hurting us or "putting us in our place." Neurodivergence, trauma, and experiences of marginalization make it more difficult to trust authority and go with the flow. Keep reading for ways to bring your Upstairs Brain to the challenge of defiance, disrespect, and other attempts at control that are driven by the Downstairs Brain.

DEFIANCE, DISRESPECT, AND THE DOWNSTAIRS BRAIN

83

Fifteen-year-old Andrew was standing by the door sharpening his pencil when Jason got in line behind him to do the same. Suddenly a scuffle broke out. When Mrs. Thompson looked up, Jason was throwing up his hands in surrender as Andrew yelled, "Back off!"

Mrs. Thompson called across the room, "Hey. Knock it off, Andrew."

Andrew glared at Mrs. Thompson. "Go F— yourself," he mumbled on the way back to his seat.

"Get out of my classroom," she said, pointing at the door.

This exchange between Mrs. Thompson and Andrew is an all-too-common occurrence. Incidents like these leave teachers exhausted at the end of each day. Instead of approaching the new morning with energy and hope, you might find yourself job hunting in the middle of the night. What if there's another option?

By this point in the book, you can probably identify that Andrew was functioning from his Downstairs Brain. What isn't yet clear is *why*. Why did Jason's innocent act of standing in line to sharpen his pencil set off Andrew's Tiger brain?

Andrew had experienced more trauma in his fifteen years than most people endure in a lifetime. His mother's trauma history led to significant neglect. He had also been sexually abused and physically attacked multiple times. As a result, his amygdala was always on high alert, even in the 10th grade language arts classroom. When Jason approached from behind, Andrew had a quick flip into defense mode. Before his Upstairs Brain could register "Jason is in line to sharpen his pencil," his Tiger brain jumped into action.

Knowing this about Andrew, what could Mrs. Thompson do differently to help de-escalate the situation?

When looking at this exchange, we can see that Andrew was acting from his Downstairs Brain, but what was happening for Mrs. Thompson? Given the high poverty rates and generations of discriminatory practices in the community, lots of students in the school had experienced trauma, and this level of agitation and violence was happening daily. Mrs. Thompson was trying to help another student when the incident at the pencil sharpener seemed to erupt out of the blue. Her Downstairs Brain leapt into protection mode. She wanted to protect Jason. She might have been worried about preserving class time or honoring the effort of the student she was currently helping. When Andrew's Tiger brain swore at her, her Porcupine brain took over. It wasn't because of Mrs. Thompson's flawed character or because she is a failure as a teacher. It's a brain thing!

What do you notice in your thoughts, feelings, or sensations as you read about Mrs. Thompson's experience?

Do you notice frustration and tension or apathy and numbness? These may be signs that your Downstairs Brain needs some additional support to feel safe, seen, and valued so that you can bring your Upstairs Brain to your students. Be sure to discuss with a trusted colleague, supervisor, or instructional coach.

BREAK FREE FROM THE DEFENSE BRAIN CYCLE

If Downstairs Brain moments naturally lead to Downstairs Brain reactions, how can we break out of this cycle of aggression, defensiveness, and self-protection? It begins with us. We must work through our triggers, so we don't end up in our reactive Downstairs Brains right when our students need some Upstairs Brain support. **That's where our power lies, in our ability to self-reflect, plan ahead, and build skills.**

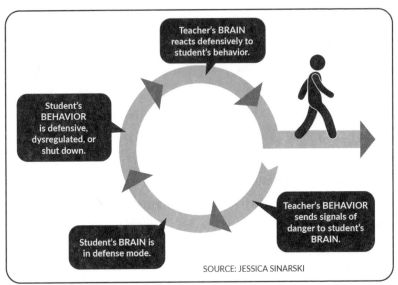

Teacher's BRAIN reacts defensively to student's behavior.

Student's BEHAVIOR is defensive, dysregulated, or shut down.

Teacher's BEHAVIOR sends signals of danger to student's BRAIN.

Student's BRAIN is in defense mode.

SOURCE: JESSICA SINARSKI

This chapter provides the strategies necessary for reducing power struggles and nurturing Upstairs Brain development in your school community. I know your job is hard, so I'll provide the language and brain-based lens to help you keep your "lid" on when you need it most, filling your toolbox for those difficult moments. Finally, we will get concrete about additional ways to help your students expand *their* Upstairs Brain potential. First, here is an easy-to-remember plan to help you disrupt the Student-Teacher Defense Brain Cycle:

1, 2, Re-Do.

Take 1 deep
BREATH.

We're a

Remember that
you and your student
are **on the same team.**

Re-Do: Support your student's ability to try again.

With patience, compassion, and maybe even a little playfulness, try one of these phrases:

- Can we re-do?
- Seems like something is bugging you.
- Can you try that a different way?
- I'm here to help.
- Let's try again.
- Want a minute to cool out?
- Do-over?
- Help me understand.
- Oops. Upstairs Brain version...

For younger students especially, you may have to give the words at first. With a kind or slightly playful tone, say something like, "Did you mean, 'Can I please finish this real quick and then come to the carpet?'" Remember, the Downstairs Brain is always on the lookout for "danger" signals coming from non-verbal communication, so be sure to relax your forehead, muster some warmth, and approach with non-threatening body posture. Practice this plan in staff meetings or with minor stuff so you're ready when the bigger Tiger and Porcupine moments come.

> *Remember, the Downstairs Brain is always on the lookout for "danger" signals coming from non-verbal communication...*

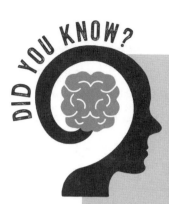

Questions can be interpreted by the amygdala as one more threat. The more you get to know your students, the better you will be able to tailor your "re-do" option to something they can hear even when their Downstairs Brain is in protection mode. Often a word or gesture or even a shoulder squeeze turns out to be much more helpful for a student in the middle of a Tiger moment than a question or long statement.

CULTIVATE MUTUAL RESPECT

Cultivating mutual respect is different from hanging some rules up and asking students to "agree." Respect and disrespect mean different things to everyone, so let's get curious. Take your time answering the questions below and then talk it through with your colleagues.

I feel respected when...

What did respect look like in your family, school, and community?

How did you learn the expectations around respect as a child?

I find it easier to show respect when...

I feel disrespected when...

When you were younger, when/why did you behave disrespectfully?

This exercise is an important starting point. Part of the challenge with getting along in the school setting is that we are a diverse bunch of people with varying needs and distinct interpretations of the same situation. Set yourself up for success by cultivating mutual respect together in your classroom community. I promise it will be time well spent.

Set Classroom Expectations Together

For younger students, use simple language. Wendy Turner shared how she updated norms the week after spring break. After a connecting activity like a fun morning meeting or game, she asked students to use just one word to "name a norm they'd like to see in our space." The results show the common ground that exists if we make space for students to name it. Plus, this process of creating norms together gets more parts of the brain involved, which helps students integrate classroom expectations in a way that just being told does not.

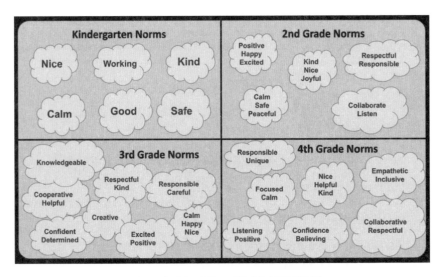

SOURCE: @MRSWENDYMTURNER ON TWITTER

With older students, try expanding the conversation to include these four categories:

- Teachers respecting students
- Students respecting teachers
- Students respecting students
- Respecting self and our space

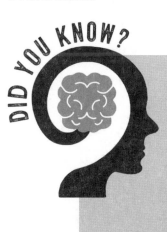

To help all students have a voice, try using sticky notes. Students write their ideas on sticky notes, and then you work together to notice patterns and categories that you all agree on.

USE AND COACH HEALTHY COMMUNICATION STRATEGIES

DID YOU KNOW?

From a neuroscience perspective, an aggressive call for kids to "Look at me when I'm talking to you!" is one of the quickest ways to send a brain into defense mode. While many see eye contact as a sign of respect, direct eye contact can set off the amygdala alarm, especially if the eyes are angry or dismissive in any way.

After a recent workshop, I was chatting with a 4th grade teacher named Maria who shared that she had been diligently working with her students on building stress management skills. They were centering their practice on the following phrase: **stress is a sign that something I care about is at stake.** My face lit up. Yes! The stress response is communicating that your body and brain are paying attention to something.

I jotted the phrase down on a scrap of paper and tucked it in my purse. It jostled around there and in my mind over the next few weeks. I noticed that my kids bickering was stressing me out because I care about raising kids who can communicate their needs and be kind to others. I felt stressed about a writing deadline because I care about keeping my promises and creating a worthwhile final product. It seemed like Maria was onto something!

Best I can tell, the thought-provoking quote seems to be a spin on Kelly McGonigal's words in *The Upside of Stress*: "Stress happens when something you care about is at stake. It's not a sign to run away—it's a sign to step forward." As I continued mulling it over, I decided to introduce the concept to my kids, ages 9-14. We started using it like this when big emotions were on the rise:

1. Check in with yourself before you blame, shout, or bark at someone (or right after if you didn't catch it in time).

2. What are you concerned about? Dig down to what you care about or what is worrying you.

3. Say it out loud.

Sound cheesy? Maybe. But it worked! Both my older boys spontaneously shared with me the following week that this way of communicating had saved them from some arguments.

- "HURRY UP, *insert brother's name said in utter annoyance*!" became "I'm concerned that we won't be on time to school if you don't move faster."

- Loudly tattling or complaining about someone else's screen time became "I'm worried I won't get as much screen time as my brother."
- "MOM—" (stretched to a five-second word) "—he's touching my stuff!" Changed completely. I overheard an exchange that went like this:
  - Brother 1: "I care about my stuff, and I'm worried you're gonna break it when you touch it without asking me."
  - Brother 2: "That's fair."
  - Brother 2 then leaves stuff alone.

In hindsight, it makes sense. Stress triggers Downstairs Brain activation, which wants power and control. Enter Tiger moments and power struggles galore—amongst siblings or between parent and child or teacher and student. But if we notice how that desire for control is tied to care and concern, which live in the Upstairs Brain, we have a chance to communicate about it more effectively.

How could this look with your students or staff? Think of a recent moment of tension and write down the care or concern that may have been underneath.

How will you teach your group about this concept?

CHOOSE SUPPORT OVER CONTROL

Kindergarten teacher Mindy Hall tries to give her students choice in their seating arrangements. Some students need additional support to find a spot where they can learn and thrive. It would be easy in a moment of frustration to jump to, "That's it! Assigned seats!" Instead, Mindy asks her students, "Are you being successful here?" With kind support instead of harsh control, she then offers to help them find a spot where they can be successful.[84] This nurturing way of enforcing consequences is especially important for students who have spent time in The Mistrust Cycle and might be more likely to interpret correction as rejection.

We should also be careful not to call out students in front of the class, as this is a quick way to activate the Downstairs Brain. I was visiting a 5th grade classroom last year to share a little bit about foster care and adoption. There are some difficult themes in that big topic, and I noticed that as some students were asking great questions, one boy was making jokes and distracting friends. I felt my well-practiced protection mode want to kick in against this student. After all, he was making it difficult for the kids who wanted to learn and grow. Catching my Downstairs Brain in action and thinking on the fly, I said to the group, "This can be tough to talk about, and it's hard to stay on task. Sometimes we want to get silly."

As we split into smaller groups, I made sure I mustered some kindness in my eyes and said quietly to him, "If it's too hard to focus in this group, we can try a different group." I kept my Upstairs Brain engaged, and he was able to get back on track. This was a kid having a hard time, not willfully giving me a hard time. Choosing support over control saved me from a power struggle and prevented disrupted learning for the whole group.

As your students' capacity to make wise choices grows, support their Upstairs Brains by prompting them to think ahead and then reflecting on how their choices worked for them. For example, before you head out for lunch, give a kind reminder: "Alright everyone, I need you guys to be thinking about what part of your brain is on. What tools or strategies are you going to use to make the most of your time?" Remember to check back in right after, helping them to reflect with questions like: "How did your plan work out? What do you want to keep or change for next time?"

TEACH FOR TRUE LEARNING

With all the education research out there, what do we *really* know about what works and what doesn't to enhance student achievement and learning? The book *Neuroteach: Brain Science and the Future of Education* aims to answer that question. Pulling from decades of research about how students learn best, authors Glenn Whitman and Ian Kelleher created "The Unconscionable List" of practices that teachers should *not* be doing.[85] So, what are the top three things a teacher should never do again?

1. Pop quizzes for a grade.
2. Starting a class by going over homework.
3. Ending a class by teaching all the way to the bell.

Other items on the no-no list include primarily delivering content through lectures, assessment dominated by tests, always being the "sage on the stage" instead of the guide by your side, and not recognizing the connection learning has with emotion, identity, and health. I'm guessing there are items on this list that you are doing in your work. Just in case your Downstairs Brain is kicking into defense mode, I'll offer this friendly reminder: we can change our practices! It starts by being honest with ourselves. Take a moment to reflect.

As I reflected on Whitman and Kelleher's list, I was reminded of how messy learning is, even in adulthood. As a professional development provider, I'm aware that it is easy to gravitate toward a polished, entertaining keynote. Participants might walk away with a great anecdote, a good quote, or an idea to bring back to their work, but the real change happens in the deep dives, small groups, and self-reflective moments. True learning is hard work. It is usually messy and often uncomfortable.

Dr. Louis Deslauriers has been examining this phenomenon for more than 15 years. In 2019, he led a study that measured the impact of passive instruction (highly polished lectures) and active learning (instruction utilizing student engagement

> *Actual learning and feeling of learning were strongly anticorrelated.*

with the material) on two outcomes: actual learning and perceived learning.[86] The findings help explain why it can be so difficult to veer away from traditional, albeit outdated, teaching styles. Deslauriers et al. found that "Actual learning and feeling of learning were strongly anticorrelated."[87] In other words, while a smooth lecture or moving keynote might give the impression of teaching a lot, tests of actual learning show that active teaching strategies are more effective.

Performance vs. Perception

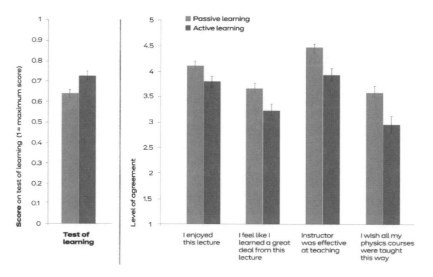

SOURCE: *MEASURING ACTUAL LEARNING VERSUS FEELING OF LEARNING IN RESPONSE TO BEING ACTIVELY ENGAGED IN THE CLASSROOM* BY DESLAURIERS, L. ET AL. (2019)

Whitman and Kelleher provided a list of research-informed practices to help teachers and administrators update their teaching methods.[88] Here are the top three research-informed strategies every teacher should be doing with every student:

1. Design classes with an understanding that students will recall the first and last moments most.

2. Give frequent low-stakes formative assessments of learning (instead of relying only on high-stakes tests that evaluate rather than inform student learning).

3. Provide opportunities to reflect on learning and performance.

I am happy to report that their whole list aligns well with what you have been learning in this book, including the call to help students get to know their brains, the need for choice in learning, and the power of play in school.

As you read items from this list, what is one teaching practice you already do that you want to keep?

What surprises or challenges you?

KEY TAKEAWAYS

- Breaking the Student-Teacher Defense Brain Cycle begins with us. It's natural that your Downstairs Brain may want to go into control mode with frustrating student (or staff) behavior. Check in with yourself: am I trying to control this person or support their development?

- Set classroom expectations together to cultivate mutual respect.

- Say hello to your stress—it's a sign that something you care about is at stake. Check in with yourself before you blame, shout, or bark at someone (or right after if you didn't catch it in time). Dig down to what you care about or what is worrying you and say it out loud. For example:

  - I am concerned about having enough time for fun stuff when students are not paying attention during the lesson.

  - I care about having a community that is kind to each other.

  - I'm concerned about whether you will get through with your work since you are talking with a friend instead of writing your answer.

- Connect and redirect privately. No one likes to be embarrassed in front of others, especially teens.

- Real learning is active and messy. Create space for students to provide input and reflect on their education.

LOW-STRESS STARTING POINT

Practice and use 1, 2, Re-Do.

Download and practice "1, 2, Re-Do" with a colleague and/or in the classroom.

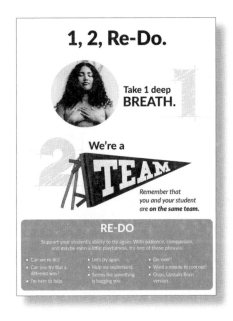

LIGHT UP THE LEARNING BRAIN

LEAD WITH THE BRAIN IN MIND

We desperately need more leaders who are committed to courageous, wholehearted leadership and who are self-aware enough to lead from their hearts, rather than unevolved leaders who lead from hurt and fear.

– Brené Brown

Perhaps like me, you have seen some training about the brain, mental health, or trauma swing the pendulum so far to understanding kids' feelings that we aren't helping them gain the skills and mindsets they need to succeed in the real world. In contrast to permissiveness, the high nurture I have been advocating throughout this book helps to create an environment where high expectations can be met. Put another way, it's not relationships *or* rigor. It's relationships *and* rigor.

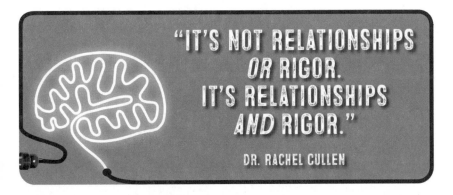

"IT'S NOT RELATIONSHIPS OR RIGOR. IT'S RELATIONSHIPS AND RIGOR."

DR. RACHEL CULLEN

BE A BRAIN-BUILDING LEADER

This final key will help you put all the pieces together, thinking about the whole child/teen as well as *your* brain and body. When our Downstairs Brain is running the show, we want to control behavior so we can teach. Of course teachers want to teach! But I also know you want students to learn. To do that, we need to become brain-building leaders in the classroom and beyond.

Survival Brain Teaching Is...		Brain-Building Leaders...
Stress. Stress. Stress.	→	Model stress management and self-regulation
No time for fun	→	Can play and be playful
Labeling students	→	Use strengths-based thinking
"Sit still and listen."	→	Get the senses involved
Command and demand	→	Connect and redirect
Catching misbehavior	→	• Notice the good • Coach for skill building
Power struggles	→	• Solve problems collaboratively • Use and coach self-reflection
"Get out of my classroom!!"	→	(1) Take a deep breath (2) Remember we're on the same team (Re-Do) Offer a do-over
"They should know better."	→	Ask "What is the need?"
Fear of judgement and change	→	• Know it's good to ask for help • Seek and act upon constructive feedback
Goal: Control behavior so I can teach.	→	Goal: Light up the learning brain!

Find more practical strategies ahead for continuing the shift from teaching in survival mode to leading with the brain in mind.

BE THE BOSS OF YOUR BRAIN

Between stimulus and response there is a space, and in that space lies our power and our freedom.

– Viktor Frankl, *Man's Search for Meaning*

I'll admit, I can be kind of intense. Mostly in a good way, I think, but I would definitely be described as "Type A." I love having an active mind, so when I started practicing yoga to help with some stress management, it was a stretch for me (no pun intended) to move slowly and notice my breathing. Toward the end of most yoga classes the instructor guides the group into a time of stillness, where you lie on your back in "corpse pose" or *savasana* [shuh-VAH-suh-nuh] for a few minutes. At the time, I was a working mom of two young kids and did not see the point of this last five minutes of class. As the group transitioned to lie down on their mats, I transitioned out the door. Not only did it feel like a waste of time, but stillness without distraction was difficult.

SOURCE: HTTPS://CHOPRA.COM/ARTICLES/WHY-SAVASANA-IS-THE-HARDEST-YOGA-POSE

Some of you reading this know what a terrible *faux pas* I was committing. After sneaking out session after session, I finally stuck around one afternoon to ask the instructor what the big deal was with this last pose. She explained that this was a time to let my body absorb the benefits of the work I had just done and that it would help me know what rest and stillness feel like. That, in turn, would help me find a sense of calm control more easily when I felt stressed or overwhelmed.

My active little brain was intrigued. Amid potty training one kid, nursing another, navigating all the illnesses of that first year of daycare, and working with clients' intense trauma histories in my therapy practice, a sense of calm control sounded nice. *Savasana* became part of my practice, and while I don't always keep up with yoga, I have found that doing guided mindfulness exercises with an app also helps. In fact, after a 2-week stretch of 10 minutes of meditation each day, my resting heart rate dropped 10 points!

DID YOU KNOW?

Breath work is good for your physical health too, with benefits like a stronger immune system, less inflammation, balanced blood pressure, and a reduction in addictive behaviors.[89]

As I learned more about the brain and body in the decade that followed my sheepish exits from yoga class, I came to appreciate both the difficulty and importance of moments of stillness. There's a reason cartoon Dora the Explorer's refrain, "Let's stop and think" was important, not just for my 3-year-old son, but also for me. It literally takes time for signals to make it from your amygdala to your higher brain regions. The more you "practice the pause" through meditation, yoga, breath work, or any other mindful exercise, the stronger you make the "staircase of your mind." That way, your "Act Without Thinking" team doesn't end up running the show all the time. Practicing the pause helps students too! Schools that have effectively implemented mindfulness programs report improved attention, reduced suspensions, and fewer office referrals.[90,91,92,93]

IT LITERALLY TAKES TIME FOR SIGNALS TO MAKE IT FROM YOUR AMYGDALA TO YOUR HIGHER BRAIN REGIONS.

What has been your experience of trying to practice the pause?

SEE THE BRAIN STATE BEHIND THE BEHAVIOR

It was Tuesday just before 4pm when my office doorbell rang. Just like every Tuesday, I heard Jacqui's mom's voice through the intercom, "We're here to see Miss Jessica."

"Come on up," I answered as I buzzed them in, a little nervous about which side of Jacqui I would see this lovely summer day.

Jacqui and her family began seeing me for therapy about a year and a half earlier. At the initial appointment, Mom shared that Jacqui seemed to be angry all the time. Dad said, "She can't even do the same chores her younger siblings do, and when we try to work on it, she just shuts down." I started as I often do, by helping Jacqui's parents understand the brain and building up curiosity, compassion, and connection-seeking in their Upstairs Brains. Then, I worked hard to create a safe and secure relationship with this dynamic third grader I had heard so much about. I used a lot of the tools I've shared with you in this book. We got the senses involved. We worked on stress management and self-regulation playfully, with loads of curiosity and safety, but it was still usually behavior coming from Jacqui's Porcupine brain that I saw in my office. Chameleon moments were common at school, and her parents were still seeing lots of Tiger and Turtle moments at home. So, what was going on?

Jacqui's Downstairs Brain protectors had grown strong very early in life. In fact, it started *in utero* when her first mom was in an abusive relationship. Jacqui entered foster care just as she prematurely entered life outside the womb, a terrified little newborn without a "safe big critter" to stay by her side as she adjusted to the harsh lights, beeping alarms, and sterile environment of the neonatal intensive care unit (NICU). Though her adoptive parents entered her life just a week later, Jacqui's nervous system had already experienced The Mistrust Cycle in ways that would have a lasting impact.

> *In fact, it started in utero when her first mom was in an abusive relationship.*

For children who have been adopted, "birth parent" or "first parent" are terms often used when talking about a child's biological mom and dad. Ideally adults begin to use whatever term the child uses. For Jacqui, it was just "Mom." Her adoptive mom was also "Mom." Confusing? Yes, but also honoring of her experience.

As she got off the elevator that sunny Tuesday afternoon, it looked like today would be much the same. Little did I know, it was about to get worse. I was using all my brain-based strategies, when suddenly she hurled one of my mindful moment toys across the room, shattering it. I was baffled. The Tiger moment seemed to flare out of nowhere. After a little de-escalation, I ended the session feeling discouraged. I was using all the brainy therapeutic tools I knew, and it felt like we were getting nowhere.

> *I was using all the brainy therapeutic tools I knew, and it felt like we were getting nowhere.*

"I don't get it," Jacqui's mom said when I checked in with her later that week. "She always looks forward to seeing you, asking, 'Is it Tuesday yet?'" she said, imitating 11-year-old Jacqui's happy voice. Then I had an epiphany!

When the next Tuesday rolled around, I was ready for that adorable, grumpy kiddo walking into my office. Jacqui, her mom, and I sat around a table getting ready to play a game. I passed out the cards, and with conversational lightness in my voice and warmth in my eyes, I said, "So I was thinking about how sometimes it's hard to be here and talk about stuff, but Mom said you tell her you're looking forward to coming. I think I figured it out!" I let the mystery build for a moment, making sure I had sparked a little Upstairs Brain curiosity in Jacqui. "You like me! And you know I care about you, and that is *really* uncomfortable." I saw the left edge of Jacqui's mouth turn up in a smile, even as she looked down at the cards in her hand.

Our relationship changed after that day. There was more space for us to talk about how hard it is to trust people, how "feelings are gross," and how she could keep getting to know what her nervous system needed so her Downstairs Brain protectors wouldn't have to work so hard. I'm not saying I never saw Porcupine spikes again, but in that moment, Jacqui felt profoundly safe, seen, and valued.

When we see the brain state behind the behavior, we hold the complicated truth that there are fears and hurts we don't see.

"So she just got away with breaking your stuff?" Nope. With heaps of safety and compassion for her Downstairs Brain, we repaired our relationship. She then used some of her savings to replace what she broke.

SELF-HARM

STEALING / HOARDING

SEXUAL ACTING OUT

SABOTAGING RELATIONSHIPS

YELLING

IRRITABLE / PRICKLY

What We See

"NOT TRYING"

SHUT DOWN / STUCK

POOR SOCIAL SKILLS

LYING

RUNNING AWAY

DEFIANCE \ NON-COMPLIANCE

HURTING OTHERS

NOT RESPONDING

SURVIVAL

SUPERFICIAL CHARM

TRAUMA

SCARED

HURT

FEELING UNWORTHY

FEELING BROKEN

"I HAVE TO SURVIVE ON MY OWN"

HISTORICAL TRAUMA

"I'M THE WORST"

LACK OF SAFE RELATIONSHIPS (AT SOME POINT)

SHAME

SENSORY DISCOMFORT

FEELING UNLOVED

FEELING WORTHLESS

GRIEF

What We Don't See

FEELING ALONE

Even when a student is rejecting you or breaking your stuff, there is more to the story, especially when we are dealing with the aftermath of trauma.

LEAD WITH COMPASSION

The school year had just begun, and five-year-old Kristie's behavior in the classroom was already out of control. Her extreme Tiger moments included pushing over shelves, screaming, biting, and running out of the room. Then Turtle brain would kick in, sending her to hide under tables and chairs. Fortunately, the principal got curious. Ms. Morgan soon learned that this brilliant little girl was found strapped into a car seat in the closet at age three. Not only had she suffered extreme neglect, but there was violence and constant danger in the home due to her parents' drug addiction. After a few days in the hospital, she moved in with her Aunt Janet. On top of managing a stressful job and two other kids at home, Janet pursued the mental health support that Kristie needed given her traumatic history, but the transition to kindergarten was rough.

Ms. Morgan worked hard to keep her Upstairs Brain engaged with this scared and sometimes scary little girl. She sought support from a local agency to help her teachers get the training they needed to deal with these extreme behaviors. She also recognized Kristie's intense need for safe and secure relationships and made it a priority to become that person. When Kristie's Downstairs Brain was ramping up, she would cool off in Ms. Morgan's office. Transitions were especially hard for Kristie, so Ms. Morgan started using small transitional objects like a little bracelet or small stuffed animal from her office to help Kristie feel connected to her when it was time to go back to class.

Ms. Morgan worked with the school counselor and Kristie's teacher to keep putting on a brain-based lens, being curious about patterns and triggers that might set off Downstairs Brain escalation as well as what helped Kristie feel safe and able to learn in the classroom. In collaboration with Aunt Janet, the team changed routines, gave sensory breaks, and supported transitions with an emphasis on her safe relationships. They also upped the educational interest for Kristie. While her behavior was severely impacted by her trauma history, testing revealed that she was academically gifted and above grade level on most measures. Not only was she stressed, but she was also bored. Over time, visits to Ms. Morgan's office decreased, Tiger moments became less frequent and less intense, and this courageous kid's Upstairs Brain was able to shine through.

This is compassion in action. This is choosing to be a brain-building safe adult, seeing the brain state behind the behavior, and being the boss of your brain. Kristie will continue to need support to strengthen those foundational building blocks of learning even as her academic skills and capacity grow. Thankfully, she has some "safe big critters" to help her along the way, adults who are leading with the brain in mind to help Kristie the Brave be successful in the classroom and beyond.

SUPPORT YOUR BRAIN WITH SELF-COMPASSION

You have been practicing self-compassion throughout this book. According to researcher Kristin Neff, Ph.D., self-compassion involves three components:

1. Kindness toward oneself, even when we suffer, fail, or feel inadequate

2. Common humanity, which means we recognize that suffering is a shared human experience instead of getting stuck in isolation

3. Non-judgmental awareness of your experience, neither ignoring your pain nor drowning in it[94]

Does any of this sound familiar? Maybe it reminds you of all those pesky reflection activities I keep asking you to do to check in with your brain and body? My hope in writing this book is to make it a little easier to notice what *is*, see the bigger picture, and find our way through.

GRIEF, GRATITUDE, AND GRIT

One concrete practice I began using a few years ago is a short journal prompt.

This could also be in a notes app in your phone, a folder in your desk drawer, or an excel spreadsheet if that's more your style. Find a place to make three columns labeled *Grief*, *Gratitude*, and *Grit*. Then get curious with yourself. What's on your mind? What is weighing you down? What's worth celebrating? As thoughts come to mind, write them down in the column where they fit best. For example, maybe you're feeling some sadness about a tough situation a kid is facing or a long-standing loss or challenge in your own life. My grief column often repeats. That's how grief works.

Sometimes the same thing fits in all three columns. For example, I am grateful for time with my kids over summer break, I grieve my expectations of the blissful, harmonious time it would be, and I notice all the gritty little details of parenting my amazing goofballs this summer.

It's really hard to keep your Upstairs Brain engaged when a kid is lying, breaking your stuff, or hurting other students. That takes grit. Pat yourself on the back for continuing to show up, for choosing Upstairs Brain responses, and for the little stuff that just takes perseverance, like putting in a load of laundry or helping your daughter with her homework when you would rather collapse in a heap on the couch. Grit, baby! Write it down. I'll celebrate with you!

I often use this practice when my heart is heavy or I'm feeling unsettled in some way. An unexpected outcome and part of what keeps me coming back to it is that as I let both my sadness and my hard work take up space on the page, it creates space for gratitude to grow. I regularly find that my gratitude list is longer than expected, not because I am denying my feelings, but because I am facing them. That mindful awareness, with kindness, helps awaken some connection to the bigger picture and the bright spots even in a difficult day (or season of days). I hope you find as much self-compassion in this simple practice as I have.

KEY TAKEAWAYS

- It is important to practice pausing, perhaps with meditation, yoga, or other mindfulness practice. It takes time for signals to make it from the amygdala to your higher brain regions.

- Extreme behaviors are usually a sign of a brain in distress. Use the iceberg graphic in this chapter to help you keep the brain in mind, especially when dealing with the aftermath of trauma.

- Remember that no one *is* their worst moment. No one *is* a Porcupine or Turtle, but we all have Downstairs Brain moments.

- Instead of punishing the Tiger or Chameleon within our students (or ourselves), support that scared part of the brain with the language and principles you learned in this book.

- When we acknowledge our grief and our hard work, gratitude and peace have space to emerge.

LOW-STRESS STARTING POINT

Choose one way you will "practice the pause" every day this week. Mix and match from the examples below or choose one and stick with it every day.

- Do the "Grief, Gratitude, and Grit" journal exercise from this chapter.

- Follow along with a meditation app like Smiling Mind, Insight Timer, or Healthy Minds Program.

- Go for a mindful walk or run without your phone or earbuds, intentionally noticing the sights, sounds, and other sensations around you.

- Add to the list of "good things" in your life that you started (see page 137).

- Pause several times throughout the day to check in with your shoulders, breath, and face:
  - Roll your shoulders forward, up, and around, letting them settle down your back.
  - As you do that, breathe in deeply, pause, and slowly blow all the air out of your lungs.
  - At the end of your long exhale, let your face relax. Release any tension in your forehead and temples, allowing a slight smile to form.
- Before leaving your classroom, think of a difficult moment from the day and get curious about the brain state behind the behavior—yours, the student or staff member, and anyone else involved. Jot a couple notes to yourself about what the Downstairs Brain protectors involved might be sensing and see if that brings some additional compassion for yourself and the other people involved.

CONCLUSION

Change is hard on the brain, but it's also the only way progress happens. I have found that approaching change with the engineering design process in mind helps me keep my Upstairs Brain engaged. While the full cycle according to NASA involves seven steps, this condensed version sticks in my head well and gets me where I need to go: ASK - DESIGN - TEST - IMPROVE

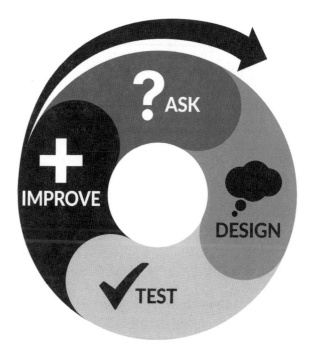

Maybe you have done things the same way for years, but you're finding it's not working. Get curious! Maybe the same skills that work for 80% of your students don't work for the other 20%. Do some research and ask for help. Try out the brain-based strategies contained in these pages (and in the digital downloads). You are a valuable brain builder.

I'm so glad we're in this together!

Glossary

Amygdala: A small group of neurons in the limbic system sometimes referred to as the emotional center of the brain, "alarm system," "traffic director," or "watchdog"

Anchors: The habits, memories, sensations, thoughts, or actions that help our nervous system experience safety and connection

Belonging: Feeling appreciated, valued, accepted, and treated fairly within an environment[i]

Chameleon Moment: People-pleasing, perfectionism, or other anxious behavior coming from a protective Downstairs Brain state

Co-Regulation: Warm, responsive, soothing interactions between two people[ii]

Culture: The norms, values, beliefs, traditions, and rituals of a group built up over time

Default Mode Network: A front-to-back connection in the brain that is active when someone is given no task to perform; when activated with safety, this system supports both self-reflection and thinking about another person's inner world[iii]

Deficit Thinking: A distorted lens focused on weaknesses, characterized by blame and lack of self-reflection[iv]

Diversity: The state of being diverse; variety

Downstairs Brain: The lower part of the brain made up of the brain stem and limbic system that is responsible for basic functions like breathing and heartbeat as well as primal emotions and the fight, flight, freeze, and feign death responses; sometimes called "survival brain," "defense mode," "the reptilian brain," or "protection mode"

Dysregulation: When an individual's ability to manage and tolerate overwhelming emotions is compromised because the brain's cognitive state and body's emotional state are out of sync due to a real or perceived threat[v]

Equity: Fairness; justice; it is not about everyone getting the same thing (equality) but recognizing that we must make adjustments where we find injustice or unfair disadvantages

Fawn: A term used to describe the survival response characterized by people-pleasing and perfectionism; has a subservient connotation that many trauma survivors do not appreciate

Felt Safety: The deeply personal, primal, and automatic response to your brain's repeated scans for signs of safety and danger outside your body, inside your body, and between you and the people around you

Fetal Alcohol Spectrum Disorders (FASD): A group of physical, behavioral, and learning conditions that can occur in a person who was exposed to alcohol *in utero*

Fight or Flight: An activated state accompanied by sensations like increased heartrate, tightness in the chest, or tunnel vision as the body prepares to battle or run away from a threat, whether real or perceived

Formative Assessment: A measure, evaluation, or indicator that is used to monitor student learning so that adjustments can be made for improved outcomes; usually brief and low stakes

Freeze: A combined state of fight-or-flight activation and immobility sometimes referred to as "deer in the headlights"

Glimmers: Small moments that spark joy, happiness, peace, or a sense that the world is okay, even for a fleeting moment[vi]

Implicit Bias: A form of bias (attitudes, behaviors, and actions that are prejudiced in favor of or against one person or group compared to another) that occurs automatically and unintentionally, that nevertheless affects judgments, decisions, and behaviors[vii]

Marginalization: Treatment of a person, group, or concept as insignificant or peripheral

Mindfulness: Living in the present moment; characterized by non-judgmental awareness and acceptance of one's thoughts, sensations, and experiences

Nervous System: Network of connections that includes the brain, spinal cord, and nerves extending throughout the body

Neuroception: The ability of the nervous system to detect cues of safety and danger; frequently detects perceived or potential threats, such as rejection, embarrassment, or fear of failure

Neurodiversity: Individual differences in brain functioning regarded as normal variations within the human population[viii]

Neuron: Brain cell that sends and receives messages

Neuroplasticity: The ability of the brain to form new connections and prune old ones that are no longer needed

Polyvagal Theory: Theory developed by Dr. Stephen Porges that helps us understand how the nervous system processes information through three hierarchical states

    Ventral Vagal: Safe, steady, and connected in an upstairs brain state

    Sympathetic: Activated, fight-or-flight, and/or distressed in a downstairs brain state

    Dorsal Vagal: Shutdown, immobilized, and/or disconnected in a deeply downstairs brain state

Porcupine Moment: Irritability, negativity, or guardedness that comes from a protective Downstairs Brain state

Post-Traumatic Growth: The personal strength, closer relationships, and other areas of development that someone might experience following a crisis or traumatic event[ix]

Post-Traumatic Wisdom: Using your experiences to understand yourself and others more deeply[x]

Privilege: A special right, advantage, or immunity granted or available only to a particular person or group[xi]

Racism: A belief that race is a fundamental determinant of human traits and capacities and that racial differences produce an inherent superiority of a particular race[xii]

Racist (adj): of, relating to, or characterized by racism[xiii]

Safe and Secure Relationships (aka Attachment): A deep and enduring emotional bond that connects one person to another across time and space[xiv]

Safe Big Critter: Used in the *Riley the Brave* series, this term refers to a trusted adult in a child's life who cares for them and helps them feel safe[xv]

Self-Compassion: Being warm and understanding toward ourselves when we suffer, fail, or feel inadequate, recognizing that suffering and personal inadequacy is part of the shared human experience, and taking a balanced approach to our negative emotions so that feelings are neither suppressed nor exaggerated[xvi]

Self-Regulation: Regulation of attention, emotion, and executive functions for the purposes of goal-directed actions[xvii]

Sense-Interoception: This sense relies on messages from the skin and internal organs to provide the brain with critical information for everyday life, such as pain, hunger, and temperature; also involved in understanding emotional cues, such as tightness in the chest when anxious or increased heat when angry

Sense-Proprioception: Receiving information from receptors in your muscles and joints, this "body sense" plays a critical role in planning our movements and what we often think of as self-control

Sense-Vestibular: This sense of movement and balance detects the head's position through tiny receptors in the inner ear providing important information that helps us feel safe and secure

Serve-and-Return Interactions: Back-and-forth volleys of communication, both verbal and nonverbal, about everyday life that demonstrate interest in a child's world

Social-Approach/Engagement System: A set of circuits in the nervous system that supports our ability to connect with other people[xvii]

"Staircase" of the Brain: A metaphor for the neural connections needed for signals to reach the Upstairs Brain for thoughtful response instead of automatic reaction

Stress Management: Constantly changing cognitive and behavioral efforts to manage specific external and/or internal demands that are appraised as taxing or exceeding the resources of the person[xix]

Tiger Moment: Fight-or-flight actions like yelling, posturing, or violence

Trauma: Any experience in which someone is not sure they have the resources to survive

Trauma-Informed Practice: Approaching people with the awareness that what happened to you is important (that it influences your behavior and your health) and then using that awareness to act accordingly and respond appropriately[xx]

Triggers: Cues of danger or threat in the environment detected by the Downstairs Brain with or without conscious thought

Turtle Moment: Thoughts, feelings, and actions—or the lack thereof—originating from the protective immobilization state of the Downstairs Brain

Upstairs Brain: The upper, outer portion of the brain (cerebral cortex) that is responsible for many complex functions such as planning, creative expression, problem-solving, self-regulation, perseverance, advanced social skills, goal-directed action, and play

Glossary Reference

i   Cobb, Floyd and John Krownapple, *Belonging Through a Culture of Dignity: The Keys to Successful Equity Implementation* (San Diego, CA: Mimi & Todd Press, Inc., 2019).

ii   Healy, Ginger, *Regulation and Co-Regulation* (Chattanooga, TN: National Center for Youth Issues, 2023).

iii   Baylin, Jonathan and Daniel A. Hughes, *The Neurobiology of Attachment-Focused Therapy* (New York, NY: W. W. Norton, 2016).

iv   McClure, Byron and Kelsie Reed, *Hacking Deficit Thinking: 8 Reframes that will Change the Way you Think about Strength-based Practices and Equity in Schools* (Highland Heights, OH: Times 10 Publications, 2022).

v   Healy, Ginger, *Regulation and Co-Regulation* (Chattanooga, TN: National Center for Youth Issues, 2023).

vi   Sara M Moniuszko USA Today, "'Glimmers Are the Opposite of Triggers. Here's How to Embrace Them.," USA TODAY, March 29, 2022, https://www.usatoday.com/story/life/health-wellness/2022/03/23/glimmers-opposite-triggers-mental-health-benefits/7121353001/.

vii   "Implicit Bias | SWD at NIH," n.d., https://diversity.nih.gov/sociocultural-factors/implicit-bias#:~:text=What%20is%20implicit%20bias?,retaining%20a%20diverse%20scientific%20workforce.

viii   "Definition of Neurodiversity," in Merriam-Webster Dictionary, November 8, 2023, https://www.merriam-webster.com/dictionary/neurodiversity

ix   Tedeschi, R.G. and L. G Calhoun, "The Posttraumatic Growth Inventory: Measuring the Positive Legacy of Trauma." *Journal of Traumatic Stress* 9, no. 3 (July 1996): 455–71. https://doi.org/10.1002/jts.2490090305

x   Perry, Bruce. D. and Oprah Winfrey. *What Happened to You? Conversations on Trauma, Resilience, and Healing* (New York, NY: Flatiron Books, 2021).

xi   "Privilege Definition & Meaning | Dictionary.Com," in Dictionary.Com, September 17, 2020, https://www.dictionary.com/browse/privilege.

xii   "Definition of Racism," in Merriam-Webster Dictionary, August 18, 2023, https://www.merriam-webster.com/dictionary/racism.

xiii   "Definition of Racist," in Merriam-Webster Dictionary, August 18, 2023, https://www.merriam-webster.com/dictionary/racist.

xiv   Stafford-Brizard, K. B., *Building Blocks for Learning: A Framework for Comprehensive Student Development* (Center for Whole Child Education, 2016). Retrieved from www.turnaroundusa.org

xv   Sinarski, Jessica, *Riley the Brave's Big Feelings Activity Book: A Trauma-Informed Guide for Counselors, Educators, and Parents* (London, UK: Jessica Kingsley Publishers, 2023).

xvi   Neff, Kristin, "The Three Elements of Self-Compassion," Self Compassion, 2023, https://self-compassion.org/the-three-elements-of-self-compassion-2/

xvii   Stafford-Brizard, K. B., *Building Blocks for Learning: A Framework for Comprehensive Student Development* (Center for Whole Child Education, 2016). Retrieved from www.turnaroundusa.org

xviii   Baylin, Jonathan and Daniel A. Hughes, *The Neurobiology of Attachment-Focused Therapy* (New York, NY: W. W. Norton, 2016).

xix   Stafford-Brizard, K. B., *Building Blocks for Learning: A Framework for Comprehensive Student Development* (Center for Whole Child Education, 2016). Retrieved from www.turnaroundusa.org

xx   Perry, Bruce. D. and Oprah Winfrey. *What Happened to You? Conversations on Trauma, Resilience, and Healing* (New York, NY: Flatiron Books, 2021).

Notes

1. EAB, "Breaking Bad Behavior: The Rise of Classroom Disruptions in Early Grades and How Districts Are Responding," District leadership Forum, 2019, https://pages.eab.com/rs/732-GKV-655/images/BreakingBadBehaviorStudy.pdf?alild=eyJpljoiU3BvSHAwbGZrMXJ5N3lcL20iLCJ0IjoiRW0xOHZyTTc1eWtSR01LdStkZjkzdz09In0%253D

2. Siegel, Daniel J. and Tina Payne Bryson, *The Whole-Brain Child: 12 Revolutionary Strategies to Nurture Your Child's Developing Mind* (New York, NY: Delacorte Press, 2011).

3. Baylin, Jonathan and Daniel A. Hughes, *Brain-Based Parenting* (New York, NY: W. W. Norton, 2012).

4. "Brain Architecture," Center on the Developing Child at Harvard University, August 20, 2019, https://developingchild.harvard.edu/science/key-concepts/brain-architecture/

5. "Brain Architecture," Center on the Developing Child at Harvard University, August 20, 2019, https://developingchild.harvard.edu/science/key-concepts/brain-architecture/

6. TED, "Molly Wright: How Every Child Can Thrive by Five | TED," August 9, 2021, https://www.youtube.com/watch?v=aISXCw0Pi94.

7. Comedian DJ Pryor, "Kingston's Conversation with Me over next Season," June 7, 2019, https://www.youtube.com/watch?v=AY35eXTKVLY.

8. Pavao, Joyce Maguire, *The Family of Adoption* (Boston, MA: Beacon Press, 2005).

9. Prizant, Barry. M., *Uniquely Human: A Different Way of Seeing Autism* (New York, NY: Simon and Schuster, 2022).

10. Nicole Baumer Md MEd, "What Is Neurodiversity?," *Harvard Health*, November 23, 2021, https://www.health.harvard.edu/blog/what-is-neurodiversity-202111232645.

11. Aherne, Daniel. *The Pocket Guide to Neurodiversity* (London, UK: Jessica Kingsley Publishers, 2023).

12. McClure, Byron and Kelsie Reed, *Hacking Deficit Thinking: 8 Reframes that will Change the Way you Think about Strength-based Practices and Equity in Schools* (Highland Heights, OH: Times 10 Publications, 2022).

13. Weir, Kirsten. "A Hidden Epidemic of Fetal Alcohol Syndrome," *Monitor on Psychology* 53, no. 5 (July 2022). https://www.apa.org/monitor/2022/07/news-fetal-alcohol-syndrome

14. Office of the Surgeon General. "Our Epidemic of Loneliness and Isolation: The Surgeon General's Advisory on the Healing Effects of Social Connection and Community," 2023 https://www.hhs.gov/sites/default/files/surgeon-general-social-connection-advisory.pdf

15. Office of the Surgeon General. "Social Connection — Current Priorities of the U.S. Surgeon General," U.S. Department of Health and Human Services. 2023. https://www.hhs.gov/surgeongeneral/priorities/connection/index.html.

16. Seigel, Daniel. *Pocket Guide to Interpersonal Neurobiology*, Norton Series on Interpersonal Neurology (New York, NY: W.W. Norton & Company, Inc., 2012).

17. Perry, Bruce. D. and Oprah Winfrey. *What Happened to You? Conversations on Trauma, Resilience, and Healing* (New York, NY: Flatiron Books, 2021).

18. Centers for Disease Control and Prevention. "About the CDC-Kaiser ACE Study |Violence Prevention|Injury Center|CDC," n.d., https://www.cdc.gov/violenceprevention/aces/about.html.

19. Harris, Nadine Burke. *The Deepest Well: Healing the Long-Term Effects of Childhood Adversity* (New York, NY: Harper Collins, 2018).

20. Bethell, Christina, Jennifer Jones, Narangerel Gombojav, Jeff Linkenbach, and Robert Sege, "Positive Childhood Experiences and Adult Mental and Relational Health in a Statewide Sample: Associations Across Adverse Childhood Experiences Levels," *JAMA Pediatrics* 173, no. 11 (2019):e193007. doi:10.1001/jamapediatrics.2019.3007

21. Crandall, AliceAnn., et al. "ACEs and counter-ACEs: How Positive and Negative Childhood Experiences Influence Adult Health," *Child Abuse & Neglect* 96, (2019). Retrieved from https://doi.org/10.1016/j.chiabu.2019.104089.

22. Baglivio, Michael and Kevin T. Wolff, "Positive Childhood Experiences (PCE): Cumulative Resiliency in the Face of Adverse Childhood Experiences," *Youth Violence and Juvenile Justice* 19 no. 2 (2020): 139–162. Retrieved from https://doi.org/10.1177/1541204020972487

23. Tedeschi, R.G. and L. G Calhoun, "The Posttraumatic Growth Inventory: Measuring the Positive Legacy of Trauma." *Journal of Traumatic Stress* 9, no. 3 (July 1996): 455–71. https://doi.org/10.1002/jts.2490090305

24. Perry, Bruce. D. and Oprah Winfrey. *What Happened to You? Conversations on Trauma, Resilience, and Healing* (New York, NY: Flatiron Books, 2021).

25. Olivera, Lisa, *Already Enough: A Path to Self-acceptance* (New York, NY: Simon and Schuster, 2022).

26. Jessica Sinarski, LPCMH, "It's a Brain Thing!," February 4, 2020, https://www.youtube.com/watch?v=BUtLZE1UB8g.

27. Young, Karen, *Hey, Awesome: A Book for Kids about Anxiety, Courage, and Being Already Awesome* (Brisbane, Australia: Hey Sigmund Publishing, 2020).

28. Pounds, Dwayne, "Partnership for a Drug-Free America 'This Is Your Brain on Drugs' PSA (1987)," September 14, 2013, https://www.youtube.com/watch?v=o5wwECXTJbg.

29. Stafford-Brizard, K. B., *Building Blocks for Learning: A Framework for Comprehensive Student Development* (Center for Whole Child Education, 2016). Retrieved from www.turnaroundusa.org

30. Turnaround for Children, "Building Blocks for Learning - Center for Whole-Child Education (Turnaround for Children)," Center for Whole-Child Education (Turnaround for Children), January 16, 2020, https://turnaroundusa.org/what-we-do/tools/building-blocks/.

31. Miller, Lucy Jane, *Sensational Kids: Hope and Help for Children with Sensory Processing Disorder* (New York, NY: Perigree, 2014).

32. https://www.britannica.com/science/information-theory/Physiology

33. Sanchez, Horatio, *The Poverty Problem: How Education can Promote Resilience and Counter Poverty's Impact on Brain Development and Functioning* (Thousand Oaks, CA: Corwin, 2021).

34. Perry, Bruce. D. and Oprah Winfrey. *What Happened to You? Conversations on Trauma, Resilience, and Healing* (New York, NY: Flatiron Books, 2021).

35. Yogman, Michael, Andrew Garner, Jeffrey Hutchinson, et al; AAP COMMITTEE ON PSYCHOSOCIAL ASPECTS OF CHILD AND FAMILY HEALTH, AAP COUNCIL ON COMMUNICATIONS AND MEDIA, "The Power of Play: A Pediatric Role in Enhancing Development in Young Children" *Pediatrics* 142, no. 3 (2018):e20182058

36. Waldinger, Robert and Marc Schulz, "The Lifelong Power of Close Relationships," *WSJ*, January 13, 2023, https://www.wsj.com/articles/the-lifelong-power-of-close-relationships-11673625450.

37. "Instagram," n.d., https://www.instagram.com/reel/CrzBFnaAgDu/?utm_source=ig_web_copy_link&igshid=MWQ1ZGUxMzBkMA==.

38. McClure, Byron and Kelsie Reed, *Hacking Deficit Thinking: 8 Reframes that will Change the Way you Think about Strength-based Practices and Equity in Schools* (Highland Heights, OH: Times 10 Publications, 2022).

39. Sanchez, Horatio, *The Poverty Problem: How Education can Promote Resilience and Counter Poverty's Impact on Brain Development and Functioning* (Thousand Oaks, CA: Corwin, 2021).

40. Daniels, Emily R., *The Regulated Classroom: "Bottom-up" and Trauma-informed Teaching* (Peterborough, NH: Here This Now, LLC., 2021).

41. Sanchez, Horatio, *The Poverty Problem: How Education can Promote Resilience and Counter Poverty's Impact on Brain Development and Functioning* (Thousand Oaks, CA: Corwin, 2021).

42. Class Critters, "On This Squirrel Scale, How Do You Feel Today?" Facebook, n.d., https://www.facebook.com/classcritters/photos/pb.100063650494596.-2207520000./347298179968092/?type=3

43. Parris, Sheri and Christian Hernandez, "The Benefits of Play in Cognitive Development," n.d., https://child.tcu.edu/play/#sthash.YyGbODUr.dpbs.

44. Willis, Judy, "What You Should Know About Your Brain." *Educational Leadership* 67, no. 4 (2009).

45. "Stress Relief from Laughter? It's No Joke," Mayo Clinic, September 22, 2023, https://www.mayoclinic.org/healthy-lifestyle/stress-management/in-depth/stress-relief/art-20044456.

46. Porges, Stephen W., *The Polyvagal Theory: Neurophysiological Foundation of Emotions, Attachment, Communication, and Self-regulation* (New York, NY: W. W. Norton & Co., 2011).

47. Dana, Deb, *Polyvagal Flip Chart: Understanding the Science of Safety*, Norton Series on Interpersonal Neurobiology (New York, NY: W. W. Norton & Co., 2020).

48. Dana, Deb, *Polyvagal Theory in Therapy: Engaging the Rhythm of Regulation*, Norton Series on Interpersonal Neurobiology (New York, NY: W. W. Norton & Co., 2018).

49. Sara M Moniuszko Usa Today, "'Glimmers' Are the Opposite of Triggers. Here's How to Embrace Them.," USA TODAY, March 29, 2022, https://www.usatoday.com/story/life/health-wellness/2022/03/23/glimmers-opposite-triggers-mental-health-benefits/7121353001/.

50. Dana, Deb, *Polyvagal Practices: Anchoring the self in safety* (New York, NY: W. W. Norton & Co., 2023).

51. "Lives in the Balance," n.d., https://livesinthebalance.org/.

52. Greene, Ross W., *Lost & Found: Unlocking Collaboration and Compassion to Help our most Vulnerable, Misunderstood Students (and All the Rest)* (Hoboken, NJ: Jossey-Bass, 2021).

53. Clint Pulver, "Inspirational Video- Be a Mr. Jensen- MUST WATCH!!," May 4, 2017, https://www.youtube.com/watch?v=4p5286T_kn0.

54. St. Romain, Dan, *Positive Behavior Principles: Shifting Perspectives and Aligning Practices in Schools* (Chattanooga, TN: National Center for Youth Issues, 2020).

55. Holley, K, "What is the Best thing About Your Kid?" Twitter Photo, August 9, 2022, https://twitter.com/KHolleyEdS/status/1557141499300683777

56. Baylin, Jonathan and Daniel A. Hughes, *The Neurobiology of Attachment-Focused Therapy* (New York, NY: W. W. Norton, 2016).

57. Souers, Kristin and Pete Hall, *Fostering Resilient Learners: Strategies for Creating a Trauma-sensitive Classroom* (Alexandria, VA: ASCD, 2016).

58. Cobb, Floyd And John Krownapple, *Belonging Through a Culture of Dignity: The Keys to Successful Equity Implementation* (San Diego, CA: Mimi & Todd Press, Inc., 2019).

59. Purvis, Karyn. B., David R. Cross, and Wendy Lyons Sunshine, *The Connected Child: Bring Hope and Healing to your Adoptive Family* (New York: McGraw-Hill, 2007).

60. Porges, Stephen and Deb Dana (Eds.) *Clinical Applications of the Polyvagal Theory,* Norton Series on Interpersonal Biology (New York: NY: W. W. Norton & Co., 2018).

61. Altogether Autism, "Autism No Puzzle, Nothing Wrong with Us," *Altogether Autism*, March 28, 2021, https://www.altogetherautism.org.nz/autism-no-puzzle-nothing-wrong-with-us/.

62. Prizant, Barry. M., *Uniquely Human: A Different Way of Seeing Autism* (New York, NY: Simon & Scheuster, 2022).

63. Rowling, J. K., *Harry Potter and the Sorcerer's Stone* (New York, NY: Scholastic, 1998).

64. Cobb, Floyd and John Krownapple, *Belonging Through a Culture of Dignity: The Keys to Successful Equity Implementation* (San Diego, CA: Mimi & Todd Press, Inc., 2019).

65. "What Is Equity? | National Association of Colleges and Employers," n.d., https://www.naceweb.org/about-us/equity-definition.

66. Cobb, Floyd and John Krownapple, *Belonging Through a Culture of Dignity: The Keys to Successful Equity Implementation* (San Diego, CA: Mimi & Todd Press, Inc., 2019).

67. "Implicit Bias | SWD at NIH," n.d., https://diversity.nih.gov/sociocultural-factors/implicit-bias#:~:text=What%20is%20implicit%20bias?,retaining%20a%20diverse%20scientific%20workforce.

68. "Privilege Definition & Meaning | Dictionary.Com," in Dictionary.Com, September 17, 2020, https://www.dictionary.com/browse/privilege.

69. "Definition of Racism," in Merriam-Webster Dictionary, August 18, 2023, https://

www.merriam-webster.com/dictionary/racism.

70. Kendi, Ibram X and Nic Stone, *How to Be a (Young) Antiracist* (New York, NY: Kokila, 2023).

71. "Definition of Racism," in Merriam-Webster Dictionary, August 18, 2023, https://www.merriam-webster.com/dictionary/racism.

72. Kendi, Ibram X and Nic Stone, *How to Be a (Young) Antiracist* (New York, NY: Kokila, 2023).

73. "Race and Ethnicity of Public School Teachers and Their Students," n.d., https://nces.ed.gov/pubs2020/2020103/index.asp.

74. McIntosh, Peggy, "'White Privilege: Unpacking the Invisible Knapsack' and 'Some Notes for Facilitators,'" National SEED Project, June 14, 2023, https://national-seedproject.org/Key-SEED-Texts/white-privilege-unpacking-the-invisible-knapsack.

75. Souers, Kristin Van Marter and Pete Hall, *Relationship, Responsibility, and Regulation: Trauma-invested Practices for Fostering Resilient Learners* (Alexandria, VA: ASCD, 2019).

76. Souers, Kristin Van Marter and Pete Hall, *Relationship, Responsibility, and Regulation: Trauma-invested Practices for Fostering Resilient Learners* (Alexandria, VA: ASCD, 2019).

77. Gilliam, Walter. S., et al. "Do Early Educators' Implicit Biases Regarding Sex and Race Relate to Behavior Expectations and Recommendations of Preschool Expulsions and Suspensions?" Yale University Child Study Center (2016), accessed June 4, 2023, https://files-profile.medicine.yale.edu/documents/75afe6d2-e556-4794-bf8c-3cf105113b7c?sv=2020-08-04&se=2023-06-04T18:05:48Z&sr=b&sp=r&sig=tRQXMKBuaqdudr3cf204Q+2X+ZhBwt9Cw1plgeRPwIA=

78. Greene, Ross W., *Lost & Found: Unlocking Collaboration and Compassion to Help our most Vulnerable, Misunderstood Students (and All the Rest)* (Hoboken, NJ: Jossey-Bass, 2021).

79. Cobb, Floyd and John Krownapple, *Belonging Through a Culture of Dignity: The Keys to Successful Equity Implementation* (San Diego, CA: Mimi & Todd Press, Inc., 2019).

80. Cobb, Floyd and John Krownapple, *Belonging Through a Culture of Dignity: The Keys to Successful Equity Implementation* (San Diego, CA: Mimi & Todd Press, Inc., 2019).

81. Menakem, Resmaa, *My Grandmother's Hands: Racialized Trauma and the Pathway to Mending our Hearts and Bodies* (Las Vegas, NV: Central Recovery Press, 2017).

82. Souers, Kristin and Pete Hall, *Fostering Resilient Learners: Strategies for Creating a Trauma-Sensitive Classroom* (Alexandria, VA: ASCD, 2016).

83. Dean, Amie, *Behavior Interventions: Strategies for Educators, Counselors, and Parents* (Chattanooga, TN: National Center for Youth Issues, 2022).

84. Souers, Kristin Van Marter and Pete Hall, *Relationship, Responsibility, and Regulation: Trauma-invested Practices for Fostering Resilient Learners* (Alexandria, VA: ASCD, 2019).

85. Whitman, Glenn and Ian Kelleher, *Neuroteach: Brain Science and the Future of*

Education (Lanham, MD: Rowman & Littlefield, 2016).

86. Deslauriers Louis, Logan S. McCarty, Kelly Miller, Kristina Callaghan, and Greg Kestin G, "Measuring Actual Learning Versus Feeling of Learning in Response to Being Actively Engaged in the Classroom," *Proceedings of the National Academy of Sciences 116*, no. 139 (August 2019): 19251–19257, https://www.pnas.org/doi/full/10.1073/pnas.1821936116

87. Reuell, Peter, "Study Shows That Students Learn More When Taking Part in Classrooms That Employ Active-Learning Strategies," Harvard Gazette, September 5, 2019, https://news.harvard.edu/gazette/story/2019/09/study-shows-that-students-learn-more-when-taking-part-in-classrooms-that-employ-active-learning-strategies/.

88. Whitman, Glenn and Ian Kelleher, *Neuroteach: Brain Science and the Future of Education* (Lanham, MD: Rowman & Littlefield, 2016).

89. WebMD Editorial Contributors, "What Is Breathwork?," WebMD, April 9, 2021, https://www.webmd.com/balance/what-is-breathwork.

90. Napoli, Maria, Paul Rock Krech, and Lynn, "Mindfulness Training for Elementary School Students: The Attention Academy," *Journal of Applied School Psychology* 21, no. 1 (July 2005): 99–125. https://doi.org/10.1300/J370v21n01_05

91. Kirp, David L., "Meditation Transforms Roughest San Francisco Schools," Jan. 12, 2014, https://www.sfgate.com/opinion/openforum/article/Meditation-transforms-roughest-San-Francisco-5136942.php

92. https://www.edweek.org/leadership/opinion-inside-a-student-wellness-after-school-program/2016/12

93. Martinez, Tonnie and Yuanyuan Zhao, "The Impact of Mindfulness Training on Middle Grades Students' Office Discipline Referrals," *RMLE Online* 41, no. 3 (March 2018): 1–8.

94. Neff, Kristin, "The Three Elements of Self-Compassion," Self Compassion, 2023, https://self-compassion.org/the-three-elements-of-self-compassion-2/

About the Author

Jessica Sinarski, LPCMH is a highly sought-after therapist, speaker, and change-maker. Weaving user-friendly brain science into everything she does, Jessica ignites both passion and know-how in audiences. Extensive post-graduate training and 15+ years as a clinician and educator led her to create the resource and training platform BraveBrains. She partners with school districts and child welfare agencies around the world to unlock resilience in children and adults alike.

Jessica makes social emotional learning (SEL) practical, equipping parents and professionals with deeply trauma-informed tools. She is the author of numerous books including the award-winning *Riley the Brave* series, *Your Magic Backpack* series, and *Your Amazing Brain*. She also shares her expertise as a contributor to magazines, blogs, and podcasts. Jessica lives in Pennsylvania with her husband and three busy boys.

Questions?
Please email hello@JessicaSinarski.com

Connect with Jessica:
Social Media platforms @JessicaSinarski
YouTube @Jessica.Sinarski

Find books, additional resources, comprehensive toolkits, and more at www.BraveBrains.com

Other Books by Jessica Sinarski

A Brief Look at Jessica's Speaking Sessions

Light Up the Learning Brain

This lively session will take a fresh look at the root of "bad behavior"—in students AND staff—and the brain processes involved. Your school days don't have to be an endless cycle of frustration and dysregulation. Discover new tools based on the latest neuroscience to increase learning opportunities, reduce negative behavior, and improve school culture.

Breaking the Cycle of Defiance and Disrespect

No one likes feeling disrespected or dealing with a student's automatic "no." These hot-button behaviors frustrate teachers and overwhelm school resources, leading to broken relationships, interrupted learning, and negativity all around. While this painful cycle might feel inevitable, applying some user-friendly neuroscience can give you the power to break free.

Steady the Ship: 10 Tools for Preventing Burnout

Take some time to fill your tank! During this refreshing workshop, participants will practice brain-boosting habits that are easy to incorporate into hectic daily life. Plus, you will get some in-the-moment rescue strategies. Feel the difference in mind, body, and soul as you understand what is really happening inside, why it matters, and what you can do about it.

What Every Educator Needs to Know About the Brain

Get past the dry data and learn how to harness the science that is transforming the world of education. Popular author Jessica Sinarski will show you how to integrate this brain-building power into the classroom and beyond. Her user-friendly methods for teaching how the brain works—and why it matters!—are eye-opening, engaging, and valuable for students and staff alike.

Capturing Students' Hearts

Perhaps like many teachers you understand the power of relationship for bringing out the best in your students. But how do you reach the kids who seem closed off, resistant, or flat-out defiant? This powerful keynote bridges the divide between theory and practice by illustrating the neurobiology of why this happens and, most importantly, what we can do about it.

Trauma, the Brain, and Hope for the Weary Educator

"Trauma-informed" has become a buzzword in education, often leaving teachers with more questions than answers. Discover the hopeful side of neuroscience, with plenty of user-friendly applications for all ages. Whether you're a trauma novice or well-versed in research about Adverse Childhood Experiences (ACEs) and the brain, you won't want to miss this uplifting learning experience. *(Beginner and advanced options available)*

ncyionline.org/speakers

NATIONAL CENTER for
YOUTH ISSUES

About NCYI

National Center for Youth Issues provides educational resources, training, and support programs to foster the healthy social, emotional, and physical development of children and youth. Since our founding in 1981, NCYI has established a reputation as one of the country's leading providers of teaching materials and training for counseling and student-support professionals. NCYI helps meet the immediate needs of students throughout the nation by ensuring those who mentor them are well prepared to respond across the developmental spectrum.

Connect With Us Online!

@nationalcenterforyouthissues

@ncyi

@nationalcenterforyouthissues